CAROLYN McVICKAR EDWARDS

Illustrations by Kathleen Edwards

The Return of the
LIGHT

Twelve Tales
from Around the World
for the Winter Solstice

MARLOWE & COMPANY
NEW YORK

Published by
Marlowe & Company
An Imprint of Avalon Publishing Group Incorporated
161 William Street, 16th Floor
New York, NY 10038

The Return of the Light:
Twelve Tales from Around the World for the Winter Solstice
Copyright © 2000 by Carolyn McVickar Edwards
Illustrations © 2000 by Kathleen Edwards

Verbal renderings of stories are encouraged as long as the storyteller
expressly credits this book.

Library of Congress Cataloging-in-Publication Data

Edwards, Carolyn McVickar.
The return of the light : traditional tales from around the world for the
winter solstice / by Kathleen Edwards.
p. cm.
Includes bibliographical references(p.).
ISBN 1-56924-617-3
1. Winter solstice—Folklore. 2. Tales. I. Title.

GT4995.W55E382000
398'.33—dc21   00-056218

9 8 7 6 5 4 3 2

DESIGNED BY PAULINE NEUWIRTH, NEUWIRTH & ASSOCIATES, INC.

Distributed by Publishers Group West
Printed in the United States of America

For my grandfather, Norval Nance Edwards,
and great-aunt, Frances Robinson Dean,
with gratitude for their loving kindness,
their stories, and their nineteenth-century roots

CONTENTS

Thank you to all those writers fascinated with myth and story, whose collections and tellings have led to these; to Matthew Lore for his vision, energy, and scrupulous editing; to Terry Ebinger for her thoughtful reading; to my sister, Kathleen Edwards for her art; Michele Wetherbee for her cover design; Pauline Neuwirth for her interior design; to Sebastian Stuart for computer glitch rescue.

And praise to the sun, whose light sparks all life.

INTRODUCTION

On March 31, 1880, thousands
of people gathered in Wabash, Indiana, the first
American municipality to be lit by electric lights. Bands
played, guns fired salutes, and then the lights sprang to
life. A hush fell over the crowd. Some people groaned
and fell to their knees.

They'd moved from dark to light, and no amount of
jaded neon expectations more than a century later, can
completely obscure, even for us, the wonder of that
vigil. For we, too, whether consciously or subliminally,
even in the midst of our wildly wired lives, keep that

same vigil each year at the winter solstice.

Solstice: from the Latin *sol stetit* meaning *sun stood still*. For six days in the northern hemisphere's December, the sun ceases its southerly crawl on the horizon and appears to rise and set in almost the same spot. The ancients watched this quiet drama with drawn breath. Would the sun begin to move again? Would the light grow anew on the great wheel of life? Would life itself continue?

A few millennia and several hundred generations later, our own deepest questions, though not so literal as those of our ancestors, are nonetheless profound. Beneath our nuanced sophistications, we too, like preschoolers, hate transition. But we live on an earth where change is the only thing we can be sure of. And our silky bodies, webbed with wisdoms belied by the rushings of our twenty-first century lives, have the pacings of plants budding and light expanding. At the moment of winter solstice, we stand at the brink of external and internal change. This primordial turning of the year, both inside and out, has the tangled, branching rhythms of modern science's chaos theory. The ancients didn't call it chaos. But they personified those same meldings and shatterings in the cunning shenanigans of their tricksters who finagle the boundaries of what we know and what we don't. Now, at the winter solstice, we ask ourselves: What are the private and shared natures of our inner and outer boundaries? What is our place in the great cycle? What are the actions and restraints required of us?

Since time out of mind humans have marked the externally vital crossing from dark to light. For the perennial truth is this: Without the sun, there is no life. Green plants, those remarkable beings who are able to make their own food out of nothing but the sun's light, are food for every other being on earth, all of whom, to stay alive, must eat either green plants or other beings who eat green plants. Though we now light our world with bulbs and take for granted not only the external day but often even our food, we still make of the return of the sun's light a joyful metaphor for social and personal renewal.

But the ancient tribal peoples, less sanguine than we, fixed their collective spirits on the wholeness of the drama and included not just jubilation in their end-of-year rites. Copying the dying year, they mortified themselves in ritual sorrow, deposed or even slayed their kings, and refrained from coupling. Then, they purified themselves. They rang bells, washed with water, made new ritual objects, and killed animals who—through ceremony—had absorbed the mortification of the group. Then, in a theater of invigoration, they showed the new year how to be fertile and strong. They made celebratory couplings with each other. They staged mock combats, accompanied by stories and song, between the forces of death and life, drought and rain, the dying year and the new. Finally, the sun began to move again! Anxiety exploded into relief. The ancients drank, ate, sang, and danced. The great reciprocity between people, sky, and earth resounded once again.

Both the sun and the moon light the earth. The yearly retreat and renewal of the golden sun has a tiny allegory in the silvery rhythms the moon. Ancient humans living in small groups measured time by seasons and events and had no need to reconcile the yearly solar pattern with the lunar. But as city-states grew up, work became increasingly specialized and trade complex and far-reaching. Seasonal and event markers were imprecise calendars for business dealings and state records. Thus, tribal ritual and festivities continued, but now overlaid with the stories, customs, and calendars of the imperial governments. The new official calendars attempted to reconcile the 354–day lunar year with the 366–day solar year. The Roman calendar at first settled the problem by introducing twelve "intercalary days" at year's end, which served to bridge the lunar light cycle with the solar. The Romans celebrated the first of the intercalary days on December 25. This was Brumalia, the festival of winter solstice, and eleven wild days of Saturnalia and Opalia followed, named after and celebrated for the god Saturn and the goddess Ops. Cold, clever, passive Saturn represented the sun at midwinter, its lowest point. The last day of each week, Saturn's Saturday, represented the ending of the whole year, lying restful and quiet before the new Sun-day. The goddess Ops, giver of law and order—today little remembered except in the words opal and opulent—majestically insisted on a once-a-year overturning of her orderliness. Slaves became masters, prisoners went free, the rich gave to the poor, and every sacred right-side-up heaved upside down. People laid their bodies on the earth for Opalia, and coupled with sweetheart and stranger, so that the coming year might wax full as Opalia's opal— said to include every basic color: red, blue, yellow, green, and white—and be altogether opulent in its blessings.

The ancient European world grew fascinated with the concept of wrapping their many gods and goddesses into one. In Rome, in the first four hundred years of what we now call the common era, two major savior-religions vied for supremacy. The first savior, Mithra, the Unconquered Sun, was said to have been born of a mortal virgin on the old Brumalia, December 25. Legend had his birth witnessed by shepherds and magi, and he performed a bevy of healing miracles, including raising the dead and causing the blind to see. Before dying and returning to heaven on what we call the vernal equinox, Mithra was said to have held a last supper with his twelve disciples who represented the twelve signs of the zodiac. The Roman military establishment hailed Mithraism for its rigid discipline and vivid battle imagery.

The Christian sun god, Jesus, Light of the World, had beliefs and rites so similar to that of Mithraism that St. Augustine declared that the priests of Mithra worshipped the same deity as he. Perhaps it was Christianity's relative softness, in those early days, towards the feminine, and its roots in Judaism, with its prediction of a messiah, that finally allowed Christ's followers to seize the day. Mithraism thus became merely a tributary to the story that today shapes one of the world's major religions.

In the last half of the first millennium, the Roman Catholic Church declared December 25 to be Christ's Mass, and made of those old intercalary days of Brumalia, Saturnalia, and Opalia the "twelve days of Christmas." An earlier calendar change by the Emperor Julius Caesar had united the lunar and solar years bridged by the intercalary days into a single twelve-month year of 365 days with a leap year every fourth year. But those ancient intercalary days, the twelve days of Christmas, continued for centuries as a pocket of time filled with the old celebrations. To the old rites of greeneries, gift-giving, feasting, fire and taper, drinking, dancing, suspensions of enmity, proclamations of peace, and entertainment of friends, the Church added permutations from the German Weihnacht, the French Nöel, the Italian Natale, the Welsh Nadolig, and the Gaelic Nollag.

In 1582, Pope Gregory, still fascinated with the precise astronomy of reconciling the lunar and solar years, introduced corrections to the Julian calendar. Piecemeal, country by country, over two centuries, the Gregorian calendar replaced the Julian. Now centennial years are leap years only if evenly divisible by 400. And the day of the winter solstice falls on December 21 or 22, no longer overlapping Christ's Mass. By now, too, the age of science, newly born, had begun to crumble the ancient congruence of body, earth, and spirit. Science pinned the literal meaning of the winter solstice on its giant fact board. Religions, increasingly divorced from the earth, nonetheless continued to celebrate the yearly birth of light in poignant symbol. The Jesus story tells of the birth of the Son-sun and the Hanukkah story tells of the tiny bit of lamp oil that lit the temple for eight miraculous days. In the Hindu world, Diwali tells of the return from the dark forest of the celestial couple Rama and Sita. Thousands of lights in every village are said to guide their way. Muslims begin Ramadan, the Fast of Renewal, after the sighting of the crescent moon in the ninth lunar month. Allah is said to determine the new year's course on Ramadan's Day of Power, and the fast is broken with gifts, feasting, fairs, and the reveling of friends. The modern-day Kwanzaa draws its celebrants together around the light of community.

And we supermarket shoppers are alive in a blaze of cross-cultural sharing that the world before this time has only dreamed. We can learn from other cultures through written, spoken, and electronic media at rates and capacities that confound all previous concepts of anthropological dalliance. The synergy of new knowledge about ancient ways and increasingly worldly awareness of Gaia-ecology is transforming the teenager of science into a young adult. Fascinated by ourselves as children of a living earth, we are hungry for the symbolic riches of peoples who understood and still understand that spiritual disconnection from air, water, soil, plant, animal, moon, and sun, is as unthinkable as a finger without a hand. The spirit is creeping back into our science, and the earth back into our religion.

We await the return of the light, outside ourselves and within. Cold and darkness color and shiver the psyche. The sky turns gray. Fatally beautiful frost laces the remaining green. Rain pours. Snow drifts. We gaze at the mystery of the great cycle, full of our own deaths and births and lives. Where is the wisdom for this gateway?

Collected here, one for each of the twelve days that for so long bridged one light cycle with another, are my retellings of twelve traditional stories about light from all over the world. Not all these tales are literally about the winter solstice, though some are. But each illuminates our fundamental connection to light and its cycles of birth, death, and regeneration. Each crystalizes the significance of light's return each year.

Like vessels, the stories carry us across the stormy, flotsamy, slippery edge of night. We cross over in three different ways: by theft, by surrender, through grace. There are four stories for each kind of crossing. When our personalities clutch their old habits, the thief may have to grab what we otherwise won't let go. When our so functional egos find their orders scuttled, some other deeper self finally surrenders to the new. And then, there are those miraculous gifts, those blessings that shower down upon us.

Read the stories aloud in company, by candlelight. Play the games, make the rites, sing the songs. Revel together with the animals and the villagers. Snuggle in the egg of the dark.

PART ONE

The Theft

E NTERTAINMENT FOR MIND, funny bone, and soul, every story and myth is a window into the subtleties of the culture that made it. Taken together, the stories and myths are excursions into what different cultures share.

We can understand story and myth on many levels. Myth we can think of not in the colloquial sense of a lie, but as the story of the soul. An individual's soul story crops up in his or her night dreams. The soul of a single culture flowers in its epics and folk tales. Tales from many cultures about a single theme give us a glimpse into the soul of humankind.

The tales in this collection tell the story of the turning world. The stories are promises. By tricky hook, trickster's crook, or gentle miracle, the light will return. The change—gradual, nuanced, but complete—will come. Indeed, the stories in this book are, from one point of view, more about change than they are about dark or light. They tell the human story of standing in one place and being pulled, as the moon pulls the ocean, into another.

The Jungians have encouraged us to treat the single tale as we might a personal night dream. Fritz Perls called the personal dream an inner movie in which the dreamer is not only scriptwriter and director, but every thing and being in the story. The delightful task of inviting the story, as we might a night dream, to tell us its truth has been known to make us fall in love not only with the story but with ourselves.

In this first set of stories, the theme is theft. The Miwok Marsh Wren, in a fit of humiliation at being scorned, shoots out the sun. The kite, an enormous bird of prey, who, like the Inuit Raven, loves shiny things, snatches a girl's earring in an Orissan tribal tale. Raven, disguised as a winsome baby, is responsible for grabbing the bags in which a wizard has shut the light. And a man in another Orissan tale, despairing of being included in the group, swipes the hot black cow who milks out light.

In each tale, the status quo, represented respectively by grudging community, powerful magician, innocent girl, or oblivious community, is like the personality entrenched in its habits and defenses, blind to spacious possibility. The personality is always busy. It is making its reputation, building its stash, wanting admiration, wielding its power, enraged at the rejections and the invisibility. All else that could be, lies in the dark parts of ourselves, disowned, unexamined, pushed aside. But a deep power lies there, too. And out of the psychic collisions between the unknown self and the life flow of the universe uncoils a vast energy. Here snatches the thief's claw—perhaps in the form of a plot, an unavoidable circumstance, or a tumultuous collapse of what is. But the tricky purpose is to unseat the entrenchments and crack the certainties, opening us to the deeper-than-personality truths of ourselves and our worlds.

WHY HUMMINGBIRD HAS A RED THROAT

OLAMENTKO-MIWOK, NORTH
CALIFORNIA COAST

The Olamentko Indians of Bodega Bay, California, north of what we now call San Francisco, were one of the Miwok tribes who made their homes for thousands of years on the north coast of California and the lower slopes and foothills of the Sierra Nevada mountains. The Miwok vanished at the turn of the twentieth century when white settlers brought their diseases and took their lands. Anthropologists and mythologists, aware that a culture whose simplicity belied its richness was dying before their eyes, recorded the stories and the memories of the few Miwok still alive. Today, on sites protected and interpreted by museum curators, you can visit Miwok ghost villages set among the native nutritional and medicinal plants about which these people knew so much.

Stationary, not nomadic, the many-tribed and many-languaged Miwok peoples shared a common understanding of the mythological origins and workings of the world. All Miwok peoples told their versions of the exploits, adventures, and personalities of the first Creature People who transformed themselves into all the animals and objects of the world. All told of Coyote-Man, a trickster whose magic was almost always for the good. Humans, the Miwok said, were made of feathers, sticks, and clay.

The Hoo-koo-e-ko-Miwok tribe of Tomales Bay told the story of Sun Woman who owed her brilliance to a coat of shining abalone shells. The last surviving member of the Olamentko-Miwok told a brief, unsentimental version of this story of Tule-Wren (today called the Longbilled Marsh Wren) and Hummingbird. The story was published in 1910.

Why Hummingbird
Has a Red Throat

At the beginning, when the first people lived on the top of the great canopy of the sky, the sky had four holes in it: one in the east, another in the south, one in the west, and another in the north. The sky holes opened and closed rapidly all the time.

The first people used their magic to come down through the holes and to change themselves into all the creatures, plants, and things of the world. So, when earth people were created, they had oak trees, and flat stones on which to grind their acorns. They had reeds for houses and baskets. They learned from the sun how to shoot arrows like rays. They learned to live together like minnows swim and mice nest.

But Cha-ka, the Marsh Wren, was an orphan boy. No one liked him. The people gave Cha-ka food. Sometimes the people even gave him a crayfish to eat. But they always made Cha-ka feel like an outsider. So Cha-ka stayed under cover of bulrush and sedge grass, only appearing at dawn and dusk to ask again for more.

Cha-ka grew more ashamed, and the people grew stingier. "Get your own food, Cha-ka," they said. "We work hard. Why don't you? It's not our job to feed you, even if you are just a kid."

Marsh Wren's eyes filled with tears of anger. The white stripes over his eyebrows quivered. "If you don't feed me," he yelled, "I will shoot out the sun!"

Everyone laughed. "Yeah, right, Cha-ka. Go right ahead."

"I will!" rattled Marsh Wren.

"Do it," said the people, clearly not believing him. They turned away.

Marsh Wren did shoot out the sun with an arrow as sharp as his beak. As though it had been a bladder filled with light, the sun popped and all the light disappeared. The whole world became dark. No sun, no moon, no stars, no fire—everything was dark. The dark seemed to last for years. No one could find food because no one could see. Everyone was starving.

All this time, O-ye, the Coyote-man, was thinking about how he could get the sun and the light back again. At length he saw something way up in the eastern sky through the hole that opened and closed as fast as Woodpecker rapped on a dead tree trunk. "I think I see light!" said O-ye to himself. He squinted his eyes. Now there was no doubt. "Yes!" he exulted.

But a moment later, O-ye's tail drooped. "Now how am I going to go all the way up there to get that light?" he asked himself.

Glumly, O-ye began to pick his way through a tangle of old blackberry vines that led to his tiny stash of acorn mush. "Ouch! ooooo-Ouch!" he yelped as the thorns scratched at his nose and his soft footpads. O-ye remembered the good old days when this path had been blanketed with wet, curling ferns. The sun's beautiful light had slanted through the limbs of the gnarled live oaks, now too hidden by the dark. "Oh rots," muttered O-ye. "Rots and sots."

"Rots, yourself," answered a high-pitched voice, followed by a "vrrrrrp."

"Huh? What? Who's there?" said Coyote-man. He heard another "vrrrrrp" sound and said, "Oh, hey! Hummingbird! How's it going, Koo-loo-pe?" Coyote-man was glad to have someone to talk to.

"Vrrrrp. Same old thing, Coyote-man. Same old thing. You know that," said Hummingbird. "If we just had some light . . ."

"Yeah," O-ye agreed automatically. Then near his eyes he felt the tiny wind stirred by Koo-loo-pe's wings. Suddenly he could picture his cinnamon, purple, and green-colored little friend, wings vibrating like twin haloes. He remembered Koo-loo-pe darting through the air faster than a fish flits through shallow water. "Hey! Hummingbird! I've got this great idea!"

"Vrrrrrrrp?"

"Koo-loo-pe!" sputtered O-ye. "Guess what I just saw? Just now? Light, Koo-loo-pe, light! I saw light way up high in the sky—way too high for me to get—but you, Humminghird, you could get it in a second."

"You saw light, Coyote-man?" The little voice was incredulous. "Where? "

"Up high, Hummingbird! Really! Go look. I know you can bring it back for us."

The tiny wind of Koo-loo-pe's wings stopped for a moment. O-ye could imagine his friend hesitating. Then he heard a reassuring "vrrrrrrrrrrrrrrrp!" and he knew Hummingbird was splitting the black air in a steep climb to the top of the sky.

"It would be crrrrrrrazy not to try!" shouted Koo-loo-pe, but he was already too far away for Coyote-man to hear.

Up, up, up rushed Koo-loo-pe, until he, too, could see the dab of light blinking inside the mouth of the hole in the eastern sky. Nearer and nearer he sped, until, heart beating wildly with his own daring, he shot through the hole and tore off a piece of the blazing orange light on the other side.

"Vrrrrrrrrrp! I got it!" yelled Koo-loo-pe. He tucked the fire under his chin and hung for a moment in the air, luxuriating in the heat. But suddenly the sound of giant wings flapping filled the space around him. In a burst of fear, without even looking to see what or who might be following him, he raced back toward the hole in the sky.

Through it he flung the fire, and then he swooped

after it. All around him, the air turned pink and blue. The fire he'd carried swelled round as a puffball and sent arrows of light down to earth below. People gathered on the shores of the bay, cheering, and Coyote-man whooped and howled. Even Cha-ka, the Marsh Wren, muttered with pleasure. "Cut-cut-turrr!" he said.

Koo-loo-pe, now glitteringly graceful in the light of a new sun, sped toward his nest. His feathers shone as they had in the old days: metallic bronze-green, jewellike purple, and rich golden cinnamon. But when Koo-loo-pe modestly lifted his head to acknowledge the happiness of everyone below, the feathers on his throat against which he had carried the light were tinged a new brilliant scarlet, the color of sunfire. And so Hummingbird is marked to this very day.

THE GOLDEN
EARRING

THORIA-ORISSA, INDIA

The Thoria are Orissan tribal peoples who live south of Calcutta on the east coast of India near the Bay of Bengal. Orissa is a general name for a group of tribal peoples who actually have many different dialects and traditions (similar to the function of the words Miwok or Inuit).

The Orissa are farmers whose every facet of life is guided by ritual, dance, and song. Dancers move head, back, arms, fingers, feet; the villagers around them clap, drum, and sing. They sing songs to express everything: humor, criticism, acquisition, satire, romance, anger. In the small, beautiful, everyday spirit world of hill and forest, every passion has a music; every craft is sacred; everyone is a poet. The storyteller, like other individual personalities in a community so focused on the group, makes no effort to stand out.

The kite is a bird native to India who, like the raven, collects objects that are shiny.

THE GOLDEN EARRING

 T HE VILLAGES IN those days were lit only by fires and the web of stars in the always-dark sky. There was as yet no sun, and the beautiful Sonwari still had both her luminous golden earrings.

Sonwari gasped with pleasure when she opened the wooden box in which they lay. By flame light, she could see tiny worlds inside their spangled, wobbling pieces. She hung them in her velvet-clefted lobes, next to her full lips, where they tilted coyly beside the innocence of her face.

Sonwari had not yet met her new husband. She must now travel to his village and make a place of respect for herself in a new life, just as her mother before her had once done.

The endless dusk hid the vibrant yellow of Sonwari's sari as she plodded to her new home on the back of a cow. To give herself courage, she touched the delicate weights of the earrings as they swung against her neck. She felt determination rise in her like a cud.

The wedding dances of the new village wrapped Sonwari so quickly into her new life that not even her struggle showed. Like a fly in a web, she was bound to her husband and her new relations.

But after every sleep, Sonwari took the earrings from their box. By candlelight, she could see in them the faces of her old family she had left at home.

Then: "Sonwari!" The song to work would interrupt her reverie. Quickly, as if she were taking the old family with her, she would slide into her lobes the slim golden hooks, warmed now by her touch.

Sonwari's father-in-law was a fragile old man whose energy showed only in his stories. For Sonwari, his tales unfolded like food wrapped for safekeeping on a journey. The old man and the beautiful girl were drawn to each other. He, too, was a fly in a web, senses dulled, his strength gone. When he talked to Sonwari, he rolled tenderly the edges of her sari or held for a moment on his fingertips the small heaviness of her earrings. Sometimes they sat silent together by the fire, her head resting on his knee, one earring quiet against his blanketed leg, the other like a jewel near her throat.

One day Sonwari went to the well. As she uncoiled the rope into its depths, in the circle of fires in the village square, a fork-tailed kite with a hooked beak and long pointed wings swooped out of the night and ripped from her lobe one of the golden earrings.

Sonwari cried out. The rope slithered out of her palms, full pail emptying into the depths. Her hands flew to her ear and came away bloody. Cawing triumphantly, the bird sailed into the night sky, the earring teetering in his giant claws. Then, jagged in the prism of her tears, Sonwari could see him caught suddenly in the sparkling web of the stars. The bird flailed to burst free and the earring tumbled from his claws, hooking on a strand of the web. There it hung, glinting gold amongst the silvery white of the stars.

Sobbing, Sonwari hauled the bucket up from the well's black hole and poured its contents into her jug.

She stumbled home; set down the jug; rinsed the blood from her ear. All around her, the throb of the drumming began.

She took the remaining earring to her father-in-law, who sat wrapped in a blanket near the fire. Sonwari kneeled, shakily telling her story. The old man stroked her head.

Then he laid her earring in his papery palm, and squinted at it in the firelight. "You say he's stuck, the kite bird?" he mused.

Sonwari nodded.

"Little Sonwari," he said, "I tell you all the time what has happened already, no?"

Sonwari gulped and nodded, tilting her head to look into his kind face.

"But not now, little Sonwari. Now I tell you what will happen. That kite bird is stuck in the star web that the great spider spins across the sky." Her father-in-law chuckled and raised his voice as the drum beat grew louder. "He's like a fly up there. He can't get away. But your poor earring is growing bigger and bigger. So big, Sonwari, it will light up the world. Your earring is going to be the sun."

Even as he spoke, a strong shaft of light cut through the smoke hole and across the pair of them, running a stripe of bright yellow across Sonwari's silk sari. Sonwari searched the old man's illuminated face. The sounds of tambourines and hand clapping swelled over the beat of the drums.

"You see, Sonwari? I am right! Go. Look outside."

Sonwari ran from his side, ducking beneath the doorway and into the air. The sky outside was mauve, not black, bluing at the edges, and high above glistered a spangled, round, golden globe. By the time she'd returned from inside holding her father-in-law by his arm, the village was a choir of voices and the globe had bared itself so boldly that the sky was singing blue and the two of them could no longer look at the blaze.

RAVEN STEALS
THE LIGHT

INUIT, NORTH AMERICA

Edgar Allen Poe's raven, messenger between the worlds of the sorrowing poet and his lost Lenore, sat on the head of the Roman goddess of wisdom and croaked "nevermore!" The Inuit trickster Raven also bridges worlds. But he is as comforting as Poe's raven is dreadful. The Inuit Raven's lusty appetites and wily loyalties are the very antidotes to Poe's "midnight in December."

The largest member of the crow family, the raven is bold, gregarious, and intelligent. At home in high mountains, northern forests, rocky seacoasts, and treeless tundra, with a song that ranges from screams to whispers, the raven is a spectacular, long-winded flier who can solve puzzles and imitate other animal sounds, and who often mates for life. Both father and mother ravens feed their young.

Inuit, called Eskimo by outsiders, is the collective name for the many far northern tribal peoples of Greenland, Alaska, Northern Canada, and the islands between. In wintertime, the Inuit, despite today's conveniences of ready-made tools and electricity, face hours of darkness, gales, and dense fog. This story, in many versions, is a staple of the Inuit storytellers' comforting winter repertoires.

RAVEN STEALS
THE LIGHT

IN THE TIME before Raven made
the stars, and before Tupilak stole
the moon and the sun, everyone
lived on this side of the sky. Tupilak
was a magician with a high cone hat
and shoes that allowed him to walk miles in a single
step. Raven lived in his cozy snow hut at the edge of the
village.

One harsh winter, when the snow froze the very
earth, Tupilak put on his high cone hat and his magic
shoes. He walked up to the sky, and used his power to

cut a hole in it. Then he climbed through and built himself a house on the other side.

His wife argued with him. "What are you doing?" she cried. "All our friends are on this side of the sky. If we live on the other side, we will be completely alone!"

"You can go back and visit," he assured her.

"I don't want to visit. I want to be here right next to everyone and everything. I don't want to live alone!"

"What do you mean, live alone?" said Tupilak. "You'll be living with me! And we'll have children, and the whole thing will be much more comfortable. Why, everyone else will want to visit you!"

"But no one has your magic, Tupilak. They won't be able to come."

"Oh, probably some of them do," he said, and persisted in his plan. He carried from the first world all his magical tools. His wife, sighing with resignation, carried a stash of frozen seal meat.

After they had settled as best they could, and had even had a beautiful daughter, Tupilak could see that his wife was still sad and dissatisfied. In order to please her, he decided to steal the light. He climbed back through the hole in the sky and walked in his magic shoes straight to the top of the sky. Then into each of two strong bags, wrapping the necks of the bags tight with sinew rope, he crammed the moon and the sun. He pushed the bags back through the hole and hooked them high on the ceiling of his house, letting out the light only when he chose to do so.

Now, the world on this side of the sky had no light at all. Because Raven loved to sleep, he hardly noticed at first. Whenever he awoke and saw that it was still dark, he snuggled back into his black feathered coat and slept again. He dreamed of steaming globs of fat, of collecting bright new treasures, and of turning breathtaking somersaults.

But the people on this side of the sky were puny and tired with lack of light and food. They didn't even have the strength to wonder anymore where Tupilak and his wife had gone.

Finally, the people came to Raven and called weakly at his door. His dreams interrupted, Raven immediately thought of Tupilak. He picked his way through his hoard of the shiny things he'd already found, and poked out his head.

"Raven, the sun never comes out anymore—and there's no moon either. We're running out of food."

Raven heard the despair in their voices. "I'll bet

Tupilak's behind all this," he muttered. Out loud he promised the people that he would try to find the sun.

"And the moon," they said.

"The moon, too," he assured them.

"A pretty puzzle," thought Raven. "This is going to be a long journey." So he took as big a bag of food as he could carry and, in another bag, several good-sized rocks. Then, increasingly roused at the idea of outwitting Tupilak, Raven pulled down his beak, drew on his black-winged coat, and soared into the freezing night sky.

Whenever he needed to rest, Raven dropped a rock from his pack into the endless dark waters below. The rock changed—kerplash!—to an island on which Raven could perch, gobbling down suppers huddled in his warm feather coat, until he was ready to fly again.

Finally, he came to the hole in the sky made by Tupilak's magic. When Raven stepped through, he found himself dazzled by the sunlight on the other side of the hole, for Tupilak had let the sun out of its bag for the day. The sky was blue. A pool of water glistened, and plants poked green, red, and pink from the brown earth. Raven saw Tupilak in the distance, unmistakable in his high cone hat, soaking up the yellow heat.

Raven coughed.

Tupilak squinted. "Is that you, Raven?" he called.

"None other," said Raven.

"What do you want?" said Tupilak.

"The sun and the moon."

Tupilak laughed. "Not a chance, Raven. They're mine now."

"You're a thief," said Raven calmly.

"Takes one to know one," grinned Tupilak, and he stuffed the sun back into its bag.

"I'm going to get them back, Tupilak!" yelled Raven into the darkness.

Tupilak let out the moon and the sun several times while Raven, munching and dozing, cast about with one idea and then another trying to form a plan. Then in the midst of the sunshine, Raven was startled by the appearance of a strong, round, lovely-cheeked maiden making her way down to the pool with a water jug in her hand. Could this be Tupilak's wife? Could she possibly have grown younger in all this light? Ah! No. It must be their daughter. In fact, she carried herself with the confidence of a magician's child. Raven blinked. All at once, he knew his trick.

He quickly balled up his black-winged coat, pushed

it under a rock, and turned himself into a tiny feather floating on the still pool.

Tupilak's daughter sat dreamily at the pool's edge. Raven Feather trembled with expectation. He had a long time to wait, however, because the young woman sang softly to herself, bathed her feet and face in the pool, and then, musing and sighing, combed out her long black hair. But she dipped her jug, and Raven swirled himself inside it. His heart leapt with the perfection of the moment when the woman took from its lip a deep quaff before beginning her walk home. Jubilantly, Raven Feather slipped down her throat. His plan was working!

Sometime later, Tupilak's daughter gave birth to a huge baby boy, whose mother, grandmother, and grandfather were overjoyed. All the pent-up tenderness of these three, alone for so long on the other side of the sky, they poured into the new little boy, who, unbeknownst to them, was Raven in disguise.

His mother nursed him and played with him. His grandmother doted on him. Tupilak adored him. Raven inside his baby form was careful to cry and pester for lots of things so that his little family would get used to giving him exactly what he wanted. He bided his time, however, before he asked for the bags of light that hung from the ceiling.

One day his mother noticed a bump on the baby's forehead. "Ooooo! You've fallen, little one," she crooned, and she nuzzled him and pressed ice to the bump.

But Raven knew then that his beak was beginning to bulge, and that he didn't have much more time.

Very soon after, he cried for the moon bag on the ceiling.

"Shh, baby, shh, that's grandpa's bag," said his mother, and she dandled tasty morsels before him. Raven, of course, ate them ravenously. Pleased that her child was eating so well, she bounced him on her knee, calling forth raucous laughter from her round little boy. But soon he again began to wail, waving his chubby little hands upward, pouring out rivers of tears.

This time, his grandmother fed him, changed him, and played the bouncing game, but always his sobbing began again, his mouth gasping for air between the heaves of his chest, his little finger pointing at the bag with the moon inside.

"Papa's out," said Tupilak's daughter to her mother. "Let's let him have it. What can it hurt? It's tied tightly enough."

Tupilak's wife rolled her eyes. "It would serve him right anyway if the thing got out."

So Raven, hiccoughing with joy, was given the moon bag to play with. In seconds, the little boy's face looked round and placid as the moon itself. His mother and grandmother rocked back on their heels, enjoying the sweet silence and the happiness of their little seal pup. The minute their attention wandered, however, Raven unknotted the sinew sure as if he'd had beak and claws, clapping and screeching as the moon sailed out, bouncing through the smoke hole like a ball of blubber.

Tupilak came rushing back to the house when he saw the moon rolling through the tear in the sky. "Who touched my bag?" he bellowed, but stopped short when his wife and daughter pointed to the baby, who had ceased his chortling long enough to emit a shriek of joy upon seeing his grandfather. "Dada!" he called, and reached for Tupilak's old spotted hand.

Tupilak's face softened like a long-cooked stew. The baby cooed and patted his grandfather while Tupilak beamed with pride. The two women looked at each other and shook their heads.

Raven wisely waited, before he cried for the sun bag to play with. Then when Tupilak had settled snoring into a nap, he began his earnest howling, waving his hands as if trying to pull down the sun bag.

Tupilak woke up. "Oh, give him anything he wants," he groaned. "Just shut him up."

The two women shrugged and pulled down the sun bag. They each, with tooth and muscle, wrapped and knotted the sinew twice more.

Their closure was so effective that Raven this time could not open the bag. Knowing he must act quickly, he rested regretful eyes for a moment on his mama's back, and then sped, bag in fist, out the door. He raced to his rock and donned the black-winged cape he'd hidden underneath so long before. His beak plunged through his forehead, and Raven took bird form once again. Grasping the sun bag first in beak, then in claws, he dove through the hole in the sky and streaked away to the people, whose eyes had grown accustomed once again to the light of the moon but who still lived without the light of the sun.

Raven felt hunger pangs as he flew. On he flapped, but his stomach growled for food. By the time Raven spied the people below fishing in the crooked river by the light of the moon, his wings were trembling with effort.

"Ga, ga," croaked Raven weakly. "Give me some fish."

"Get your own fish, Raven," said the people. "We hardly have enough for ourselves."

"Please!" begged Raven. "I'll let out the daylight!"

"You don't have daylight, Raven," said the people, forgetting that they themselves had asked him to bring the sun.

Raven cawed with exasperation. He dropped the sun bag, and with his remaining strength, rammed at it three times, pecking in it tiny holes out of which sizzled particles of the sun, tumbling into the sky as sparkling spinning stars.

"He does have something in his bag!" exclaimed the people. They rushed to ply Raven with fish.

Raven gorged and sucked every bone slick. Then, full of power, he tore open the bag. Out exploded the sun, while people screamed and covered their eyes. In a very short time, they were able to bear again this stupendous light and gratefully prepared for Raven an enormous and delectable feast.

On the other side of the sky, Tupilak and his family mourned. Some say they got so lonely they came back to this side of the sky. Others say if they came at all, it was to steal the light again. But Tupilak has never been able to take the light for as long as he did that first time. Whenever it disappears and returns again, whenever people watch the moon roll into the sky among the bits of sun that are the stars, they think of Raven. And whenever people hear a baby crying, they remember Raven's trick on Tupilak.

THE SUN COW
AND THE THIEF

The Orissa have the largest variety of tribal communities on the ethnographic map of India. The Kuttia Kondh are farmers who specialize in the soulful craft of woodcarving. Like other Orissa, they have at the core of their communal strength the "village council" and the "dormitory." The dormitory is the largest hut, three-sided, open in front, hung with musical instruments, and decorated with symbols of the animal spirits. When the workday is done, it is the site for the gathering of everyone in the village for the dance. It functions as a kind of school of dance for youngsters growing into tribal traditions and it is the meeting place for the elders of the village council who make decisions affecting every social, economic, and religious part of life.

The Orissa borrow from their Hindu neighbors, and their neighbors borrow from them. The Hindu tell the story of Surya, the sun god, born from the heavenly cow, Aditi. The Hindi word for cow, go, also means "ray of dawn," or "ray of spiritual illumination."

The Sun Cow and the Thief

Back at the beginning, the village was like a hinged box with many sides. A lonely man stood on the outside looking in. Through the cracks, he could see brightly colored crisscross lines everywhere. People walked to and fro along the lines, carving shapes and painting shimmering colors as they went. The man saw an order so neat and easy it seemed he should have been able to slide right in, the very blood in his body singing. But something was wrong with him, with the way things were. He could not get in. It was as if the village had no doors. Only cracks. He could only look, never touch. He would always be on the outside, looking in.

Round the edges of the box, the Sun Cow walked. Round and round its perfect sides she walked, milking out her light in the day, filling the village box with color and warmth. At night, she chewed her cud, her black sides giving quiet warmth but no light.

The man stood between Sun Cow and the village. The only warmth that the man could touch was Sun Cow herself.

Whenever those inside the village looked out, they saw only their Sun Cow, that lovely black heat, that night-chewer, that day-maker. They smacked their lips with the cream of it. They did not say, "Look at that nice man standing outside looking in! How silly that he stands alone at the edge when we could simply make a place for him in our carvings of shapes and colors. Come, sir, you are welcome."

They didn't say that. They didn't even see him.

And so the man waited for Sun Cow every day, waited for her to pass him by. He smelled her musky flanks, saw her soft eyes, and touched her velvet hot muzzle. By some mysterious pressure, her light honey milk poured out from her udder. The man could feel the pressure of his own sadness inside him.

All at once, one day, the man decided to take the Sun Cow for himself. When all the pretty village people could not have her anymore, then, finally, everything might be fair.

So he waited for her, not even bothering to hide. The village people could not see him, after all, and she had walked sweetly near him, nonchalant, every day of his life. The day he stole Sun Cow, he simply tossed a noose over her head and pulled her away. Away over the edge of the world. Away from the box. Away from all the can't-get-in. Away alone to the edge.

The lights and colors in the village plunged into darkness. Without Sun Cow's milk there was only night. The people could not see. Babies cried, unfound and unfed by their mothers. No one knew when to wake up, when to work. All the order lay like unswept wood scraps in a dark room. The tidy lines were lumped and smudged, the colors disappeared. Where had their Sun Cow gone? What had become of her? They waited in sorrow and fear.

The thief was having his own problems. At the beginning he luxuriated in the warmth of Sun Cow's solidity, in her rhythmical grassy breath. But away from her circling walk around the little box world, away from her habits, no light came from her udder. And because she would not let him milk her, it was night for him, too. No one else had her, but now he didn't have her either.

When the thief, in desperation, tried to set beneath her a pail and squeeze her teats, she kicked the pail away with such certain force that he feared that she would kick him, too, should he persist. She was only trying to save his life, of course, for just think what would happen to a single person who tried to milk the sun!

The thief held his head in his hands. For ever so long he sat, hoping for her light again, longing for a sign that he might milk her. Finally, he knew he could not keep her anymore. He leaned against her for good-bye, for a final giving-in to going back to the endless looking in and never having. Then he slipped the noose from its stake and from over her head and set the Sun Cow free.

But she did not return to her circling walk around the village. Instead she leapt up, high, joyously high, up over the moon. And now she walks not just around one village but in a vast sky circle around all the villages, around the circle of the whole world, so that no one now need simply look in without being part, without being seen. Everywhere there are doors, carved intersections, lines crisscrossing that can be walked in and about, shivering and shining with color. Everywhere there is light.

PART TWO

The Surrender

THE THEME OF the second four stories is surrender. Sun himself must give in to the Polynesian trickster Maui's clever trap. Sun in the Miao-tzu story succumbs first to the magic of the mirror, then to the wheedling of the rooster. All the nine worlds surrender to the Norse trickster Loki's envious murder of the god of light. In the tale from Tanzania, Fly takes a leap of faith and works with his arch enemy Spider to bring the morning home.

As in the first set of stories, the status quo is stingy, parched, envious, and arrogant. We resist even knowing about the change, let alone changing. We persist in hiding from the new. We cover even from ourselves whatever it is we're convinced is unacceptable or impossible.

Something will have to be broken for us to change. WHACK! And we find ourselves giving up and giving. And through the pain and the flames, we find that Life and Stubborn Will to Live have clung to each other and that Sun's daughter is even more beautiful than she.

How Maui
Snared the Sun

Prior to 1500 C.E., the Polynesians were the most widely spread people on the face of the earth. From Indonesia they voyaged and settled the islands of the great Pacific, including Malaysia, Tonga, Samoa, the Marquesas, Tahiti, Fiji, Hawaii, Easter Island, and New Zealand. They are peoples of thirty languages and exuberant stories.

Maui, the misshapen man-bird–foster son of the gods, is the central character in a vast cycle of legends, some of which come as close to Pan-Oceanic myth as we can get. Polynesians credit this trickster with their prodigious array of navigational skills, everyday tools for gathering and preparing food, and the spunky inventiveness that colors the cultures of these peoples sometimes called "the Vikings of the Pacific."

How Maui
Snared the Sun

W HEN MAUI-NOT-what-he-seems had grown up, he left his foster father and set out to find his mother, Hina-of-the-fire, and the three brothers who lived, he knew, somewhere on the earth.

Along the way, Maui fished up whole islands from the bottom of the sea. He hid the Fire-keeper's smouldering fingernails in the tree and taught the humans to call them out of hiding by rubbing one kind of wood upon another. He tossed the sky higher than the mountains, where it stays to this day.

Maui wandered far. At last he spied his brothers hurling their spears against a huge rock in the game of *riti*. Who could bounce his spear the greatest distance? Maui watched. But when he came near, as if to join them, his first brother chortled.

"Hey! Who are you, Wrong-shape?" he yelled, pointing at Maui's twisted back.

"It's Big-foot!" razzed his second brother, pointing at Maui's feet.

"It's Bent-neck!" shouted his third brother, pointing at Maui's leaning head.

Maui answered with his spear. He shattered their rock into a thousand pieces. "I am your brother!" panted Maui, triumphant.

The brothers glanced at one another in surprise. But they looked away quickly, not wanting to show that they were impressed.

"Our brother!" hooted Maui's first brother.

"Wrong-shape thinks he's our brother!" mocked the second.

"You're not our brother!" yelled the third.

"Am so!" shouted Maui.

"Not!" shouted the brothers.

"Am!"

"Not!"

"Mother!" shouted the first brother.

Hina-of-the-fire appeared. Maui saw that she was very beautiful.

"No, you are not my son," said Hina-of-the-fire. "My sons are these three."

"Did you not have another son?" asked Maui.

Hina looked at her first three sons and then back at the stranger, her eyes growing wide.

"Did you not leave him to die at the edge of the ocean?"

All the brothers looked at Hina.

"I thought you had died," she whispered.

"I didn't die," said Maui. "My sister, Hina-of-the-sea, carried me to the jellyfish. The jellyfish took me in her long wet arms and delivered me to the gods and goddesses of the sea. Tama-nui-ki-te-rangi is my father."

Maui's brothers looked at one another. How could someone who looked like Maui-wrong-shape be their brother? And how could Bent-neck know Tama-nui-ki-te-rangi?

Hina-of-the-fire drew Maui to her and wept.

Maui's brothers were sullen even when Maui invented the trapdoor that kept the eels in their eel pots. "Old Maui-full-of-tricks thinks he's something," they said. "Says he raised the sky off the ground and gave us fire. Next he'll want to stop the sun."

Maui's jealous brothers were right. Stop the sun is just what Maui wanted to do. He got the idea from watching Hina at the pounding of her tapa bark. At work all day with her four-sided mallet, she could reach only the middle of the board by the time Tama-nui-a-te-ra, the sun, slipped back into the sea.

"Mother," said Maui, "you don't have enough time to finish your work."

Maui's brothers rolled their eyes. "There he goes again," whispered Maui's first brother. "Making good with mama."

But Hina-of-the-fire smiled. "Oh Maui, you are so right!" she exclaimed. "Tama-nui-a-te-ra makes his way so quickly across the world each day that plants and fruits take years to ripen and fishermen can barely paddle to deep water before the darkness comes again."

Maui raised his eyebrows. "I saw the gods put Tama-nui-a-te-ra on his course," he said. "Believe me, they never meant him to move this fast." Maui flexed his biceps. "Tama-nui-a-te-ra is going to change his dance, or I'm not Maui-strong-one."

The brothers had stopped pretending they weren't listening. Maui's first brother exploded. "You'll be Maui-cinder if you try to trap the sun," he jeered.

"Maui-ember!" taunted the second.

"Yeah! Maui-ash!" laughed the third.

Maui stuck out his tongue.

Hina-of-the-fire shook her head and motioned for her other sons to keep quiet. "So, Maui," she said. "You would try to trap the sun?"

"I hate to see you work so hard, Mother," said Maui. "I will make Tama-nui-a-te-ra remember that there are humans down here who need him."

"I believe you can do it, Maui," said Hina. "But you will need the magic of your grandmother. She is Ka-hu-a-ka-la and she lives in Ha-le-a-ka-la, the house of the sun. You must paddle your canoe to Ha-le-a-ka-la. There, on the mountain, beside the *wiliwili* tree, you will find the grass house of your grandmother. Ka-hu-a-ka-la rises every morning when the rooster crows and cooks bananas for Tama-nui-a-te-ra's breakfast. Three bunches she puts out; you must steal every one. Then, when she calls you, tell her you belong to Hina-of-the-fire and ask for her help."

Maui-full-of-tricks paddled through the waves and swells to Ha-le-a-ka-la. All the world rejoiced at Maui's plan.

On top of the mountain, by the *wiliwili* tree, the rooster crowed three times. Maui saw his Ka-hu-a-ka-la hobble out of her grass house. Feeling around with her hands, the old woman set out the first bunch of bananas. Maui saw that she was blind.

Maui snaked out his big hand and grabbed the bananas. Ka-hu-a-ka-la put out two more bunches. Maui stole them all.

Ka-hu-a-kala patted the ground where she had set the bananas. "Where are the bananas I cook for Sun's breakfast?" she cried out.

Maui grinned and kept silent.

The old woman sniffed the air. "I smell a man!" she called out. "Come out, wherever you are."

"You smell Maui-thief, your grandson," said Maui. "I belong to Hina-of-the-fire, and I've come to Ha-le-a-ka-la to punish Tama-nui-a-te-ra. He goes too fast across the world."

"I smell Maui-take-a-dare," said Ka-hu-a-ka-la. "Who says you can change the dance of the sun?"

"I can with your help, Grandmother," said Maui.

Ka-hu-a-ka-la sniffed. Maui could see she was pleased with his answer. "So!" said Ka-hu-a-ka-la. "You would snare the sun, is it?"

Maui nodded. Then, remembering that his grand-mother could not see him, he reached out and touched her hand. "Yes, Grandmother."

"You need sixteen strong ropes," said Ka-hu-a-ka-la. "One rope for each of Sun's sixteen legs. You must weave them from the hair of your sister, Hina-of-the-sea. Come back when you are finished and I will tell you more. Now go! I have Sun's breakfast to prepare."

Maui returned the fat red bananas to his grandmoth-er's hands. Then, deep under water, he collected the hair of his sister, Hina-of-the-sea, swirled in the bristles of her brush. Of Hina's hair he made sixteen ropes with nooses at each end. And then Maui, ropes piled in his canoe, invited his brothers to help.

The brothers were grudging.

"Oh come on!" said Maui. "With our grandmother's help, we can do it!"

The brothers shook their heads, but they came with Maui to Ha-le-a-kal-a in the darkness of the night. In the morning, Ka-hu-a-ka-la touched each of their foreheads. "You must weave a net," she said. "Like this," and she laced her fingers cunningly. "You must hide in the lap of the *wiliwili* tree—dig yourselves a hole there!" She scrambled to a joint in the mighty roots, just as if she had eyes that could see. "And then," said Ka-hu-a-ka-la, "you must wait with this magic club."

"What's the club for, Grandmother?" asked Maui's first brother.

Ka-hu-a-ka-la snorted. "You think you can take Tama-nui-a-te-ra without a fight?"

Maui took the club. The four brothers wove the net and dug the hole. They strung the net across the top of the mountain and looped it about the trunk of the *wili-wili* tree. Then they hid and waited.

In the morning, Tama-nui-a-te-ra came in a great rush through the crack in Ha-le-a-ka-la.

"Now!" Maui yelled. The brothers leapt out and, as each of Sun's legs got caught, they pulled the nooses tight and whooped.

Tama-nui-a-te-ra bellowed. He struggled and heaved. But the brothers' clever rope trap held him fast and the *wiliwili* withstood the pull of his weight.

Sun's face turned red with fury. "What do you want, puny ones?" he roared.

"You're not doing your job!" shouted Maui. "You

hurry and hurry and the people don't have light to finish a day's work. Promise to go more slowly and we'll release you."

Tama-nui-a-te-ra strained at the snare. "I'll do no such thing!" he cried, and he turned his most ferocious heat on the four brothers.

Maui's three brothers shrunk away from the terrible furnace of Sun's anger. But Maui stood up and began to swing his magic club at Sun's trapped legs.

Whack! Whack! Whack! Whack!

Maui broke four of Sun's legs.

Maui's brothers cheered.

"I will roast you alive!" shrieked Tama-nui-a-te-ra. The hairs on Maui's body singed away. His face began to blister.

Whack! Five! Whack! Six! Whack! Seven! Whack! Eight legs now Maui broke.

"Okay!" screamed Sun. "Stop! Okay! I promise to go slowly across the sky. Let me go!"

Maui and his brothers loosed the Hina-hair ropes. The rooster crowed. Tama-nui-a-te-ra turned one last furious look on his tormentors and limped away to have his breakfast.

Maui and his brothers left the ropes of their sun-trap

dangling near the crack of Ha-le-a-ka-la. "Every time he sees it," said Maui's first brother, "he'll remember his promise."

Maui's brother needn't have worried. We sometimes see the Hina-hair ropes of the sun-trap streaming out of Ha-le-a-ka-la. They look for all the world like the legs of Sun.

But Sun could not have forgotten his promise, even if he'd wanted to. It's true that half of every year, Tama-nui-a-te-ra moves as quickly as he always did on his eight good legs. But the other half of the year, he scuffles slowly on his eight broken legs. Then the people have Maui-full-of-tricks to thank for the sunshine that ripens the plants in their season and makes time for the pounding and drying of the tapa and the spearing of the fish.

HOW THE COCK
GOT HIS CROWN

MIAO-TZU, CHINA

Part of the seven percent—or seventy million people—known today as the "National Minority Peoples," the Miao-tzu of the modern southwestern provinces of Guangxi-Zhuang, Guizhou, and Yunnan are the descendants of the original peoples of China. The Miao-tzu's roots are multitribal, each tribe having kept distinctive region, costume, customs, and dialect. Like the Tibetans, the Miao-tzu have resisted for centuries assimilation into the majority culture of the Han. The Miao-tzu and the Chinese have fought brutally, the Miao-tzu tenaciously guarding their own lands and customs.

Peoples who clash, of course, ultimately borrow from each other. The Han tell this same story with an emperor's wishes at its center. The tale is Miao-tzu, however, and in this version, tribes interact with one another rather than with the dynasty's ruler.

How the Cock Got His Crown

Once, long ago, when the world had just begun, there were six suns shining in the sky instead of just one. One spring, the rains refused to come, and the six brother suns parched the earth with their great heat.

The farmers of every tribe watched in great dismay as the young green shoots they had sown with such effort baked brown in the white blaze.

The wise ones of a village in the west gathered with their chieftain. The chieftain's forehead was creased with worry. "Without food we shall surely die," he said.

From within the crowd an old man said, "The only help for it is to shoot the suns."

The chieftain's forehead relaxed. "That's it!" He clapped his hands. "We must gather from all the tribes the best archers. They must shoot down the suns!"

Strong archers from every tribe in the land traveled to the village in the west. Their clothes were of many colors, and they spoke different tongues. But all were ready to rid the sky of the dangerous brother suns.

Alas! Though their bows were hefty and their arrows swift, and six times six they tried, pouring sweat and grunting with exertion, not one arrow reached even halfway to the suns.

The archers looked at one another in great humility. In their many languages, they said, "The six sun brothers are too far away for our slender arrows."

People drooped sadly in the terrible broil. "How can we save ourselves?" they wondered.

Then suddenly, Howee, a sharp-eyed warrior from a faraway tribe, had an idea. Using his hands so that he could speak to all the people, he beckoned them to the edge of a pool of still water. There, moving ever so slightly on its surface, were reflected the six balls of blinding white. Howee pointed up with one hand to the heavenly suns and down with the other to the mirrored suns. Then, smiling hugely, he drew his hands together.

Ah! Howee seemed to be saying that the suns, in sky and water, were the same!

Howee drew his bow. But instead of shooting up into the sky, he aimed straight down into the pool. His first arrow pierced the first sun, which disappeared into the bottom of the pool. Ah!

He fired again, and the second sun disappeared, then the third, and the fourth, and the fifth sun. The people whooped. Howee was shooting down the suns!

When the sixth sun saw what had happened to his brothers, he fled over the hill. The people fell at once into an exhausted sleep. They planned to wake the next day to sow again their crops.

But alas! There was no next day! For the sixth sun, frightened and angry, had hidden himself deep in a cave and refused to come out.

The night went on and on. The chieftain's forehead crinkled again with worry. The wise ones gathered. "The crops will no more grow in constant darkness than they did in too much light," said the chieftain.

"We must send someone to coax the sun from his hiding place," said the old man.

The people first sent the tiger to the sun's cave. The tiger roared and roared for the sun to come out. He batted with his paw at the cave's door. The sun was resolute. "Go away!" he shouted. "I won't come out!"

The people then thought that the lowing of the cow might lure the sun. The cow begged gently outside the cave's entrance. But the sun was still sulking. "I won't come out," he yelled again.

At last, the people sent a cock to crow outside the hiding place of the sun. The cock puffed up his feathers. He neither asked nor begged, but simply shouted exuberantly. The sun was enchanted. "What a lovely sound," he said, and peeked out to see who could be making such music.

The cock, just as pleased with his own music, strutted and crowed again and again. The sun liked Cock's sounds so much that he came all the way out of his cave. Sun and Cock bowed to each other and Sun gave Cock a present of a little red crown.

Cock wears his red crown to this very day whenever he summons the sun. And, even if the sun is slow in the cold time, remembering with sorrow the deaths of his brothers, he never fails to greet his feathered friend, nor to light the day for the farmers who are growing their crops for the people to eat.

Loki and the Death of Light

From the far northern lands of mountainous glacier, howling storms, and pathless forests, came the Vikings, a hungry, restlessly creative people who had crossed from Norway to Iceland by 840 C.E. They settled Greenland, Labrador, Newfoundland, and half the British Isles, and reached North America five hundred years before Columbus. Farmers, lawmakers, and daring explorers, the Vikings made stories that honored poets as often as warriors. Their god Odin hung himself on the world tree for nine nights and days without closing his eyes for the revelation of the magic runes' writing that would allow the stories to talk even to people not yet born. By the eleventh century c.e., an unknown poet had penned these tales in verse in the Poetic Edda; two hundred years later an Icelandic chieftan called Snorri Sturluson wrote them down in the Prose Edda.

They are haunting stories of gods and goddesses, giants, elves, trolls, and ogres; of ice-cows and fire storms, glowing plenty and appalling destruction. The great mischiefmaker, Loki, is the hinge on which swings the door between what we think we desire and what must be.

Mistletoe, scorned as "devilbane" by the Catholic Church, which accepted all the other greeneries of the ancient solstice festivals, grew on large, fortuitously sited trees that were still objects of worship by country folk. According to the Roman Pliny, who wrote in the first century, Druids cut and distributed this odd plant as a charm against evil. Mistletoe, called all-heal by the people, was said to avert ill luck to herds. Kissing under it, a custom we carry over from the English, seems to preserve a vestige of the license of the ancient folk festivals.

Loki and the
Death of Light

THE AIR WAS sweet in the upper world, home of the wind. The swamp wolf was caged; the eagle atop the world tree slumbered. The great serpent dozed at its roots. The watchman at the rainbow bridge relaxed in the midst of sounds of teasing, laughter, and waterfalls. Green vines entwined the great hall of the goddesses with the great hall of the gods. The rainbow bridge shimmered. The giants were far away; and the deities, every one of them, were safe.

Loki, that fire-haired pretzel of an athlete, neither god nor giant, somersaulted to cover up his envy. He landed on his feet, but his heart felt upside down. Balder again. Every single god and goddess loving that pretty boy Balder who was never anything but good, kind, fair. Every answer of his just right. Perfect, that's what Balder was, and adored for it.

This very moment, the deities encircled Balder, god of light, who stood, head thrown back, radiant, arms outstretched. They were pelting him with every sort of object, each of which fell away from his body harmless as a snowflake. On and on the deities played this strange game in self-satisfied, jubilant relief.

Just weeks before, Balder, the glorious one, had dreamed, over and over again, that he would die.

"It's about time," Loki had thought, privately. But he'd said nothing. Balder's parents, Loki's foster brother, the great magician, Odin, and Odin's wife Frigg, the fate-knower, had gripped each other anxiously, then called all the deities together. Thor had come, strutting around swinging his irritatingly accurate hammer. Bragi had begun to froth his endless poetry. Frey with his harvest of hair, and Freya with her cat-drawn chariot had brooded together while Blind Hod, god of night, Balder's shy brother, had tried clumsily to comfort Nanna, Balder's wife, who rocked, weeping, in a corner. The lot of them had been shocked, mournful, then buzzing with counsel. What could be done to prevent the death of their beloved Balder, son of light? "He simply must not die!" they shouted. "He cannot!" they roared. "We will not let him!"

They'd devised a plan. Frigg would ask every single being in all nine worlds—living and not living—to refrain from hurting her precious child. Loki had turned himself into a fly on the wall and watched while Frigg, glowing with zeal, had cloaked herself for departure.

Frigg asked water, air, fire, and metal, each in all its forms, not to hurt Balder. Beasts, birds, rocks, snakes, disease. Each one had assured her, she reported when she returned, that they would never, ever bring harm to Balder, god of light.

So now, giddily, smugly, the lot of them mocked fate, making of Balder a target because he couldn't be wounded. Peelings, stones, the golden knights and pawns of their great chess set, even arrows, made no difference. Balder's beatific participation irritated Loki all the more.

Loki changed his shape. He became an old woman. He knew Frigg would mistrust him if he went to her in his own form.

Frigg was spinning when the crone hobbled up to her. "Your Balder is in peril," wavered the crone.

Frigg looked up, frightened.

"They're throwing things at him," croaked the old woman.

"Oh! Of course," smiled Frigg, relieved. "They're playing a game with him, but he can't be hurt. I've asked every being in the nine worlds not to hurt him."

"Really!" the crone marveled. "You talked to every single one?"

A flicker of annoyance passed over Frigg's face. "Well, yes," she said. "Everyone that counts. I didn't bother with the mistletoe. It's so small and weak, it couldn't possibly make a difference."

The old woman clucked and moved slowly away. Out of sight of the goddess, Loki leapt out of the old woman's shape and into his own. Snip, snap, he's reached an oak, and plucked the mistletoe there, crooning a little song of triumph. "Too small and weak, are you, little friend? We'll see about that."

Loki carved a point on the mistletoe's thickest twig. It was soft, but Loki knew it wouldn't matter. Strange, pale weapon in his hand, he slunk back to the deities' great silly game.

He found Blind Hod, god of night, wistful, as usual, standing at the sidelines.

"Why don't you play?" asked Loki, putting his hand on Hod's shoulder.

"I've nothing to throw, and I can't even see him."

Loki gave an encouraging snort. "Aghh! You can do it! Let me help!"

Into Hod's hand he placed the dart. Then using his own body as a lever, he guided Hod's shot. The mistletoe whistled through the air and landed its point directly into Balder's heart.

The beautiful god sank instantly to his knees and then fell face down upon the ground.

The boisterous merrymaking fell deathly silent. Stunned, the gods and goddesses could not move at first. Then Nanna screamed: "My husband!"

Loki watched them, his heart gloating, but his mind unquiet.

There was nothing to be done. Balder, god of light, was dead. Hel in the world of the mists and the dead, would be keeping a place for him. All the inhabitants of the nine worlds, the elves, dwarves, the mountain giants, frost giants, and the Valkyries paraded in the great funeral procession. Moving as if made of lead, the gods and goddesses fashioned for their beloved an enormous boat. When they placed his still form on its planks, Nanna's heart burst within her. Balder's wife, then, they had to lay beside him. So despairingly weak were the deities in their sorrow, that they needed a giantess to push the boat into the sea. The orange of the funeral pyre lit the ocean with an angry, mournful light.

"Who will win my undying love?" whispered Frigg. "Who will bring my son and his wife back from Hel's underworld?"

On Odin's eight-legged stallion, Hermod the Bold galloped into the Hel's underworld. A giantess stopped him. "What are you doing here?" she asked. "Your skin has too much color for death."

"Have Balder and Nanna passed this way?" asked Hermod. "I've come for them."

"Yes, it's three days now. They are in Hel's hall."

The ghosts of Balder and Nanna smiled wanly at Hermod. They gave him gifts for Frigg and Odin. Hermod begged Hel to let them return. "The whole world mourns," said Hermod. "Nothing grows. There is neither warmth nor light. The hearts of humans and gods are dim with tears."

Interest reddened Hel's shadowed sockets. "Are their eyes, too, dim with tears?"

Hermod assured her that it was so.

"Then so be it," said Hel, her great teeth showing. "If everyone and everything on earth will weep for these two, they may return."

The ghosts of Balder and Nanna stirred hopefully.

"But if even one does not shed tears, they stay."

Hermod raced back with his wonderful news.

Everything and everyone wept. The mistletoe, especially, cried for its terrible part in the death of Balder. Ever after, the mistletoe carries the pearlike berries of its tears.

But Loki. He alone strained against his ordinary shape and took the shape of a giantess. "I do not weep," sulked Loki from inside his disguise. "He never wept for me. And I do not weep for him."

And so it was that Loki's dry eyes kept Balder in the world of the dead. The gods and goddesses, enraged, caught Loki. He'd changed himself to a salmon this time, and hidden in a pool at the side of the house with the four doors, north, south, east, and west. Odin caught him in a net and squeezed him tightly that he might not wriggle away. Ever after the body of the salmon slims toward the tail where Odin once grabbed.

The deities chained Loki to a rock. They hung a poisonous snake above him to drip venom in his face. Loki's wife, ever faithful, stood catching the poison in a bowl as it fell. But each time she left to empty the bowl, the venom fell into Loki's face. The earth trembled and shook, then, with Loki's agony.

Balder did return. But not until Loki had broken free of his fetters and loosed the swamp wolf from his prison. The great serpent at the bottom of the world tree uncoiled. The watchman at the rainbow bridge blasted his trumpet when he saw them coming. The eagle atop the world tree awoke and screamed in terror. The swamp wolf swallowed Odin. The great serpent writhed and spit flames that engulfed all the nine worlds. In a last burst of power, the sun gave birth to a daughter even more beautiful than she.

Then, finally, onto the ashes came Balder, god of light, free from the underworld, clinging tenderly to the arm of his Nanna.

And then the only two humans left in the middle world, the two who had hidden themselves away, came out into this new light. Their names were Life and Stubborn Will to Live.

The gods and goddesses, then, the ones who were left, gathered together on the sunlit plain of the upper world, home of the wind. Shyly, joyfully they clung to the returning couple, even as Life and Stubborn Will to Live had clung to each other in the middle world.

The gods and goddesses sifted through the wreckage of their great hall. In the ruins, they found the golden chess pieces with which they had once amused themselves. Slowly, slowly, they began to play again.

THE PULL-TOGETHER
MORNING

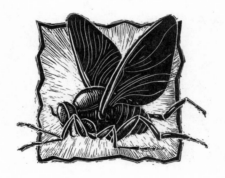

SUKUMA, TANZANIA

This story from the largest tribal culture in Tanzania could well have been a teaching story for the whole of the remarkable country which took its independence from Britain in the 1950s without the terrible tribal conflict and bloodshed that battered other freedom movements. Under the leadership of Julius Nyerere, Tanganika liberated itself in 1961; in 1963, Zanzibar joined Tanganika and became Tanzania, a combination of both countries' names. The country had never adopted the languages of the colonizers—neither German nor English—and now forged its national identity based on Ki-swahili, a lingua franca, and a concerted effort towards modernization. Nyerere, known as Mwalimu, the teacher, is remembered for his wisdom and endurance in Tanzania's great transition, his support of the African National Congress and Nelson Mandela's fight against apartheid in South Africa, and his assistance in freeing Uganda.

The Sukuma, a chiefdom formed in the 1700s, live in an area called Usukuma, southwest of Lake Victoria, the largest lake in the world. Enormous rock formations, called kopje, *punctuate the land, which feeds its people with rice, cassava, potatoes, and corn.* Shamba, *or farming, is a family activity here: Everyone works together to plant, weed, and harvest in order to make sure of enough food for the coming year. The words for creator god in Ki-sukuma, the Sukuman language, are associated with the sun. Like the great light in the sky, the creator shines the force of life onto earth. Families pray inside their homes to the gods and their ancestors, asking for strength, abundant rainfall, and prosperity.*

In this story, black represents the people of Africa; blue the color of Lake Victoria; and red, fire and life. Harambee *means "pull together" in Swahili.* Umoja *means "unity."* Imani *means "faith."*

THE PULL-TOGETHER MORNING

IN THE BEGINNING of the world, there was no sun in the sky. Everyone was falling into holes, bumping into one another, and picking a lot of fights.

Lion called a meeting of all the people. Everyone came: Giraffe, Zebra, Antelope, Monkey, Cobra. They jostled and bickered with one another for a long time before Crocodile finally got their attention.

"Listen, people!" said Crocodile. "Umoja. If we're going to solve our problems, we've got to admit that despite our differences, we're all in this together."

Antelope broke the sober silence that followed Crocodile's words. "Harambee," she said. "We've got to pull together."

"Yes!" shouted someone else. "Harambee! We've got to pull together."

The crowd repeated it. "Harambee," they chorused. "Harambee!"

Then Leopard began the problem solving. "Sometimes when it rains," he suggested, "the sky cracks open. You know how you can see a blaze of light on the other side of the crack? If only we could get to the other side of the sky and get some of that light for ourselves!"

Hyena laughed. "How are we supposed to get up there?" she asked.

"Even if we could get up there, we're too big to get through the crack," Elephant pointed out.

Mouse nudged Spider and tapped Fly's wing. "We're not too big," she whispered. Then in a loud voice she offered, "Spider, Fly, and I will try."

The people murmured hopeful approval.

"Wait a second!" said Fly. "I can't go with Spider. She'll eat me!"

"You're forgetting!" cried Monkey. "Harambee! We've got to pull together!"

"Imani," said Spider firmly. "Have faith, Fly. Why would I eat you when you're helping us all get light?"

Fly was silent, while he thoughtfully rubbed two of his back legs together.

"Harambee," said Mouse. "We've got to pull together."

"Okay," said Fly finally. "I'll go."

The big animals cheered. "And we'll stay right here and make music for you until you return," announced Lion.

"Harambee!" everyone shouted. "Harambee!"

Spider spun a silver ladder to the top of the sky. Mouse and Fly climbed carefully after her. With her sharp little teeth, Mouse gnawed a hole in the sky at the end of the ladder and the three small animals squeezed themselves through to the land of the Sky People.

They blinked and looked at one another in the new light. Mouse's whiskers bristled delicately and Fly's wings glittered purple and green. They could hear a faint surge of sound from the people below.

Spider smiled. "We did it!" she said.

"Harambee," said Mouse. "We're pulling together."

Everywhere around them in a shining grass field were the Sky People moving swish, swish, to and fro.

The Sky People questioned their strange visitors and then took Mouse, Fly, and Spider to their king. "These people want light," they told the king. "They say they've come from Earth to get it."

Now the king of the Sky People did not want to give these strangers light. But he also did not wish to appear stingy. He shifted on his throne, adjusted his bright robes, and pressed his fingertips together. "This is not a small matter," he said importantly. "I must call a meeting."

Spider, Mouse, and Fly watched as the Sky People gathered behind the vibrant black, red, and blue folds of a big tent. Fly winked at his companions, then flew toward the secret council.

The people inside talked long and seriously. But they never noticed Fly, who had taken a place very quietly on the wall. "We can't give these people light," said the king. "We'll give them a test instead. They won't be able to pass it—and then I can have them killed."

The king pushed back the beautiful cloth and Fly flew quickly to Spider and Mouse. "He's going to try to kill us," Fly whispered.

"We're going to have to pull together," said Spider.

"Harambee," murmured Mouse.

"Friends," said the king to the three small animals. "My people need grass for their roofs. You may have light if—and only if—you cut down all the grass in this field by morning." The king smiled smugly.

Mouse smiled back. "Thank you for your generosity, oh King. We will do it."

"What do you mean, 'we'll do it'?" cried Fly, when the king had gone away. "We're never going to be able to cut all that grass."

"Imani," said Spider. "Harambee."

Mouse thought for a moment. "Yes!" she said. "Harambee! I'll be right back." Mouse wiggled back through the hole in the sky and down the silver ladder. Soon she returned in the company of the Ants, who had been making music at the bottom. They marched, feelers keeping time to the drumbeats far below. "Harambee!" yelled the queen of the Ants, and by morning not a single stalk of grass stood in the field.

The king looked uncomfortable, but he pretended to be pleased. "Ah," he said. "Yes. Well, I see you've passed the first test. But now, of course," the king paused and pressed his fingertips together, "you must pass another. I will kill a cow. And you must eat all the meat by morning."

The Sky People brought basket after basket of freshly roasted meat. "Thank you for your generosity, good people," said Spider. Fly buzzed with anticipation.

"But even I can't eat all that," he said sadly, when the Sky People had gone away.

"The big animals could in a second," said Mouse.

"Yeah, but how are they supposed to get up here?" asked Spider.

"This is impossible," said Fly, sucking a bit of meat to comfort himself.

"Imani," said Spider. "Have faith, Fly."

"Hey! I've got an idea!" said Mouse.

The three friends looked at one another. "Harambee," they said.

Mouse dug long tunnels in the ground. Fly and Spider helped Mouse bury the meat in the tunnels. In the morning, not one scrap of meat lay in the baskets. Fly, Spider, and Mouse thanked the king for the delicious feast.

The king pursed his lips. He did not look happy, but he managed to smile. "Congratulations," he said. "Since you've passed the second test, I must call another meeting."

Spider and Mouse waited outside while Fly once again took his silent place on the wall.

The king was furious. "These little people are strong," he fumed. "I can see we're going to have to give them light. But I'm going to make it hard for them."

Fly buzzed back and told his friends the king's plan. "He's got two boxes," explained Fly. "The black one has darkness in it. The red box has light. He's going to make us pick."

Just then, the king burst through the curtain with the two boxes. "You must choose," he said. He narrowed his eyes and traded the boxes from one hand to the other. "Light or dark?" He raised his eyebrows and waited.

Mouse pretended to think. "Hmmm," she said. Then, quickly, before the king could change his mind, she grabbed the red box and raced for the hole in the sky. Mouse, Spider, and Fly plunged down the silver ladder into the waiting, music-making crowd below.

"They've returned!" roared Lion. "They've returned!"

"They're back!" the people yelled excitedly.

Mouse's whiskers trembled a little. "We've pulled together—all of us," she said in her loudest voice. "And we've brought you light—in this box! "

The crowd hushed when Spider and Fly pushed up the lid on the red box. But out of the box came not light at all. Instead, Rooster jumped out of the box. He picked up one foot, then the other, and rustled his feathers handsomely.

Mouse felt her cheeks grow hot. Rooster was not light! She had been tricked by the Sky King! The people began to protest.

At that moment, Rooster threw back his head. "Ha-ha-ha-ram-beeeee!" he called out. "Ha-ha-ha-ram-beeeee!" At once the eastern sky filled with color. Pink and yellow it glowed, and then the sun popped fiery red into the sky.

That's how it was on that very first golden, pull-together morning. And Rooster has been calling up the sun for all of us ever since—"Ha-ha-ha-ram-beeeee!"

PART THREE

The Grace

ND THEN, IN these next four
stories, there's the gift. The eye-watering sweetness of
honey inspires the !Kung's trickster Grandfather
Mantis. The Luhyan girl who once left her village and
locked away the light is now racing home to take off
the lids. In the Warao story, the light keeper's generosity pours through emptiness, darkness, dream,
and friendship. And La Befana from Italy changes forever her habits in honor of the Royal Child of Light
whose face might just be in the room right now before
you.

The epiphany. The showering. The umbilicus. The magic of the empty vessel. The flying even when we're standing still.

GRANDFATHER MANTIS AND HIS THINKING STRINGS

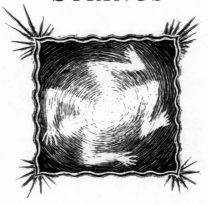

!KUNG SAN, KALAHARI DESERT

The nomadic !Kung San, who have lived in southern Africa for thousands of years, call themselves the Zhun/twasi or "the real people." Centuries ago, these hunting-gathering peoples fought fiercely for their land and their lives when yellow- and black-skinned peoples from the north and finally whites from across the sea colonized southern Africa. The !Kung San finally made their home in the desert, where no one else wanted to live. Remarkably resourceful, the !Kung feel bound to birds, insects, water pans, and animals. No part of life is untouched by the spirit world danced up at the beginning by the Creature People. All the arrows of misfortune must still be danced away in healing trances of village movement in which women's clapping and singing raises the h/um that can make the world well again.

Although the !Kung are constantly affected by drought, the overgrazing of their Bantu-speaking neighbors' cattle, and the attraction of the "easy life" of wage labor, they keep alive their profound knowledge of gatherable edible, medicinal, and toxic plants and hunt over great dis-

tances—for wildebeest, gemsbok, giraffe, various reptiles, and birds. Honey is a rare prize.

In the dry, freezing cold winter months, a number of !Kung bands may settle around one permanent spring. Trance dancing, singing, and gaming intensify. Once boastful, crabby, endearing trickster I Kaggen, Grandfather Mantis, wiggles his sweet tooth, the stories begin!

GRANDFATHER MANTIS AND HIS THINKING STRINGS

No ONE BUT the antelope knows exactly where Grandfather Mantis lives anymore. But everyone knows to thank Grandfather Mantis for Sun Man's living up high in the sky. Even before the people of the Early Race knew they were the People of the Dream, and before the Dream People were Altogether Creatures, Grandfather Mantis was old, and Sun Man was young and lived on the earth.

Sun Man rose early in the morning. He yawned and stretched out his graceful arms, spreading the fingers of his small hands. Out of his armpits streamed a great light for all the people. Grandfather Mantis rocked on his porch, soaking up Sun Man's warm, yellow light into his skinny old bones. Not so long before, the Ant People had attacked Grandfather Mantis and eaten him up. But Grandfather Mantis had used his magic to join up his bones again and to come back to life. He chuckled now to think of it and tapped the big old brown tooth in his head where all his power lay.

"Heh, heh. Forgot to take my tooth, Rock Rabbit," he said to his wife. "Forgot to take my tooth."

Rock Rabbit looked up from painting water designs on ostrich eggs. "You're a lucky old man," she said.

"Heh! Heh! So you're a lucky old woman!" chortled Grandfather Mantis, and he tapped his tooth delightedly.

Sun Man's light shone down on Grandfather Mantis's porch, on Rock Rabbit, and on Old Sister Blue Crane, who was gathering melons and berries. Grandson Mongoose played a pebble game in a knot of other children, while his mother, Porcupine Daughter, stitched together the thongs of a sandal. Her husband, Kwammanga, the Spirit of the Rainbow, lay collapsed in a hammock with his feet and arms hanging down.

Sun Man's light shone, too, over the Lion People, who slung food bags over their right shoulders and quivers of poisoned arrows over their left. Silently they hunted the springbok, who jumps high in the air when surprised.

In that distant beginning season, Sun Man's warm magic flowed over all the land. Whenever he raised his arms, it was day. Whenever he lowered them, it was night. The Bee People and the Elephant People and the Tic People loved the rhythm of Sun Man's light. Their faces crinkled with pleasure in his heat.

But inside the dreamtime, Sun Man grew old. His back grew stiff and his knee joints ached. He rose later and later each morning. He napped soon after breakfast and went to bed in the afternoon.

"What's going on here?" complained Grandfather Mantis. "I'm not getting heat anymore." Grandfather Mantis sent the Bird People to find out. The Bird People returned, rumpled and solemn. Darkness was everywhere, even though it was supposed to be daytime. "Sun Man is getting old," they explained. "This shining all the time is getting too much for him."

"Well, I'm old," snapped Grandfather Mantis. "Doesn't stop me."

His wife raised her eyebrows but said nothing.

"I'm cold, Mama," said Mongoose, Porcupine's son.

Porcupine Daughter pulled Mongoose close. "Everything is broken!" she mourned to her husband, Kwammanga.

Everyone was listless and sad.

"We cannot live this way," said Sister Blue Crane worriedly. The children pressed around her thighs for warmth.

For a long time Grandfather Mantis said nothing more, except to complain about the cold and whine because his food was not hot. Rock Rabbit shook her head. "Tji!" she said. "Complain, complain, complain. If you don't like it, Old Man, why don't you do something?"

Grandfather Mantis did not like to listen to his wife's scolding. He began to long for something sweet.

"My body needs strength," said Grandfather Mantis, "so I can listen to my thinking strings when the wind blows."

He took off his sandal and threw it hard on the ground. The sandal turned into a dog. Grandfather Mantis sent the dog to fetch him a nest of honey.

The dog came back with just one piece of honeycomb.

"This is not enough," snorted Grandfather Mantis. "My thinking strings need much more honey than this." And he sent Mongoose away to fetch him the whole nest.

Mongoose took a long time to bring the honey to his grandfather. Mantis was irritable. "Why do you take so long?" he said.

Mongoose started to speak, but Rock Rabbit interrupted. "It's dark everywhere, Old Man," she said. "Of course the child takes long to find his way."

Grandfather Mantis sucked piece after piece of honeycomb. He swallowed slowly and smacked his lips. Suddenly, a wind outside blew through the little bush hut where everyone huddled. Mantis's wings trembled. "I can hear my thinking strings move!" he cried.

The wind continued to blow, and Grandfather Mantis continued to tremble. Rock Rabbit and Sister Blue Crane looked at each other significantly.

Finally, Grandfather Mantis called Mongoose and all the other children to him.

"Go to the place where Sun Man is sleeping," he told them. "Grasp him firmly and throw the old man into the air. His armpits will open and once again we can get warm all over."

The children did as Grandfather Mantis said. They crept up to Sun Man, making no more noise than the hunter following the springbok. They stood still and waited until their eyes could make out in the darkness just where to hold Sun Man.

The children put their hands under Sun Man. He felt hot all over. Together they lifted and then heaved Sun Man into the air. Over and over he tumbled. His arms and legs opened wide to keep his balance. Hot beautiful light poured from his armpits.

"Sun Man!" Mongoose shouted. "You must go up high in the sky. You must make heat and light for us, so we will no longer be cold and so the whole earth will have day!"

Sun Man heard. He let himself grow hot as fire and let his tumbling turn him round as a ball. That day, Sun Man became a bright circle of heat up high in the sky.

Grandfather Mantis was proud. He tapped his old brown tooth. "What man is equal to me? Who but I have the magic?" Thin legs shuffling in the dust and head nodding, he began a gay and boastful dance.

Rock Rabbit looked at Old Sister Blue Crane and shook her head. How could she scold her husband when everyone was warm again and there was light to eat and work and visit by?

All that first day with the new Sun Man high in the sky, the people rejoiced. They ate their fill of meat and drank the cleanest water. They put on their finest clothes because now everyone could see one another.

When the new Sun Man went away for the night, Porcupine Daughter smiled at Kwammanga. "Everything is put back together again," she said.

The Spirit of the Rainbow smiled back. "Now is the time for the stars," he said.

THE GIRL WHO
MARRIED THE SUN

LUHYA, KENYA;
TANZANIA; UGANDA

The Luhyan people's fertile homeland, in western Kenya north of Lake Victoria, is today the most densely populated area on earth. Originally from central Africa, Bantu-speaking, and a tenth of Kenya's indigenous population, the Luhya comprise twenty-three "houses" or tribes in Kenya, Tanzania, and Uganda, each with its own dialect and customs. From 1952 to 1961, the Luhya, along with their sister tribes, initiated the Mau Mau rebellion against British rule, the first modern liberation movement of Africa, and an epic of cruelty, sacrifice, and courage.

Young Luhyan now often find jobs in the cosmopolitan Nairobi, but their roots of farming, herding, tribal tradition, and spiritual practices are strong. Elaborate celebration and ceremony for the newly dead is a time for pleasuring the ancestors. This funereal story is about the warmth and succor we gain from the spirits gone before us.

THE GIRL WHO
MARRIED THE SUN

 NE MORNING, LONG before the pounding of the maize in the mortars had begun, a girl, resolved for days not to marry a man she didn't love, sneaked away from her village. "No matter how many cattle he has," she said to herself.

By early in the evening the girl was miles into a thick forest. Finally, exhausted, she fell forward into a clearing. There, in the miserable twilight, she lay, twisted and hungry, on the ground. She was free, but she was also alone. What would become of her?

At first, the girl did not notice the rope wobbling gently above her and descending directly from the sky.

But then, suddenly, she saw it hanging like a great umbilicus above her. Hesitating, her heart pounding, she grasped it. Instantly, she was lifted into the heavens. Thump! She landed in bright daylight next to a heap of marrow-sucked bones at the edge of a strange village.

The girl felt her limbs. They were whole. The ground at this trash heap seemed solid. Satisfied, but nervous, she squatted, unsure of what to do next.

Then a regal old woman appeared. The girl cast down her eyes respectfully.

"Who are you?" asked the old woman.

"I am from a faraway village," replied the girl in a low voice.

"You are beautiful, child," said the old woman, reaching out her hand. "Stay with me. I am Sun's mother."

The girl said nothing. She imagined her family at home sitting together eating corn cakes and yams, wondering where she had gone. Tears stood in her eyes.

"Come," said Sun's mother.

The girl allowed herself to be led to the house of Sun. She found it stored with sweet potatoes, bananas, and beans. While the girl feasted, the old woman told her again how beautiful she was. "My son is chief," she said. "He will want to marry you."

The girl stopped eating. Had she escaped a forced wedding, only to be trapped again? She kept her eyes down. "I cannot marry a chief," she said politely.

Thinking the girl merely modest, the mother encouraged her. "Wait for him in the garden, child. But you must not be afraid or cry if something very red and bright appears before you."

In the garden, the girl ate a plump fig. Suddenly, the place was blinding as lightning. Sun had returned, and the girl covered her face.

Sun was enchanted with the girl's smooth dark skin. He welcomed her immediately as his new bride. The girl said nothing and did not raise her face.

Next day, Sun sent his chief servant, Moon, to speak to the girl. Moon told her of Sun's warmth and kindness. "How honored Sun would be to take you into his family," said Moon. The girl was silent.

For the next six weeks, Sun continued to send servants to talk to the girl. Evening Star told her how happy the other wives of Sun were. Morning Star told her how rich was Sun's land. The girl would not reply. She only ate, and thought, and dreamed. And she watched Sun from a distance.

But even when Sun sent her something of all that grew in his land, the girl was not yet ready to speak.

Finally, in the seventh week, Sun decided to give her his own rays. He took them to the girl himself along with a huge, smooth pot. The girl's heart was pounding. She took Sun's rays and put them into the pot.

Then the girl opened her mouth. Her face was shining. "I will marry you, Sun," she said.

The people in the land of Sun sang and danced and grew fat at the wedding feast.

In time, the girl, now a young woman, had three children. She grew to love them and her husband, his wives, and her mother-in-law. Unbeknownst to her, however, her happiness was not matched on Earth. For Sun's rays, shut away in the giant pot, no longer shone in the world below the sky.

One day, the young woman made plans to visit her family. "For three days only, my beloved," said Sun, "I will let you go." Sun dropped another rope out of the sky, on which the woman and her servants clung, laden with presents.

The woman's family was huddled by a fire when she

arrived. Hardly recognizing her, they were amazed to see her. They had given her up for dead long before. From her mode of travel, they saw immediately that she was no ordinary daughter. So they sacrificed not an ordinary ox but one of perfect white. They poured a portion of its blood at their spirit-daughter's feet; they roasted the rich meat; and all the people, heavenly and earthly, ate their fill.

The woman and her family rejoiced, the unspoken stories of years pouring out of their mouths. "Oh daughter, we would be completely happy," said her parents, "if only we had light as we did before you were lost."

But at the end of three days, when the woman and her servants made ready to return to heaven, the rope caught them up so quickly that she had no time to say goodbye.

Full of sorrow and joy at once, the woman rushed to the pot in which she had hidden away her husband's rays. She snatched off the lid, and brilliant light once again showered Earth below.

"All my family and all my village, my husband," she said, "are happy at the return of your day."

Sun looked tenderly at his young wife. "Then I will send my servant to light the night sky, too."

And so it is to this very day that Moon serves not only Sun but also Earth.

THE LIGHT
KEEPER'S BOX

WARAO, VENEZUELA

The Warao, of the equatorial Orinoca River delta, build their houses on stilts to avoid annual flooding. The Spanish explorer Alonso de Oieda named their country Venezuela—little Venice—after their networks of river homes. As late as 1850, despite more than three centuries of Spanish colonialization, the Warao still worshipped the life in every being on earth. Today they work with other native peoples to build into Venezuela's constitution civil rights for themselves as separate cultures.

In this story of offerings, the Warao preserve a remnant of their ancient "gift culture" in which the giving away— rather than selling—of parts of the selves of plants, animals, and people is the bloodlike circulation that forms community. Gift culture—versus what anthropologists call "commodity culture"—moistens the spirits of all beings with generosity and cooperation.

In a world teeming with spirits, even a simple box woven of itiriti *leaves is alive with dream and vision. The* itiriti *plant, teach the Warao, is a gift from the body of a primordial ancestor. "Let us borrow empty vessels," said*

Meister Eckhart, the thirteenth century German mystic. The itiriti *box could be such a vessel, pouring out the spaciousness into which the new can flow.*

THE LIGHT
KEEPER'S BOX

AT THE BEGINNING of the world, by the waters of the Orinoco River, there was no day. The people had only wooden torches to light their villages. By the flicker of their fires, neither day nor night truly existed.

In the midst of one village lived a chief with two daughters. News came to the chief of a man somewhere who kept the light. The man called to his older daughter and said, "Go and see where this young light keeper is, and bring some light to me." Then he blew on her face so that the *hebus* of the bush, water, and sky might leave her safe.

The young woman, wearing her most lovely *mauritia* apron, packed herself a small sack, and left. Just outside the village she found many roads on which to travel. She didn't know which one to take. The one she finally chose led her to the house of Deer. He greeted her with his soft eyes and his antlers like fuzzy tree branches above his smooth ears. She stayed with Deer a long time, laughing, talking, and loving with him. When at last she returned to her father, however, she did not have the light.

The father decided to send his younger daughter. "Go and see where the young light keeper is, and bring some light to me." He blew on her face. "I will play my flute for you, too," he said.

The young woman combed out her hair and set off. She, too, came to the many roads and could not decide which one to take. But she heard the faint sound of her father's flute, and a feeling about the roads crept over her. They seemed to have faces, and she chose the one that seemed strong and old. Finally, after much walking, she came to the house of the light keeper.

The light keeper's face was as young as the road had

seemed old. "I have come to meet you," she said, "and to get from you some light for my father."

"I have been waiting for you," the light keeper answered. "Now that you have arrived, come stay with me."

The young man took up a box, made of tightly woven *itiriti* leaves, that he had at his side. Carefully, so that the dreams inside would not spill out, he opened it. The light colored his sinewy arms brown and his teeth white. It poured a sheen over her black hair and dark eyes.

And so the young woman discovered light. After showing it to her, the young man closed the lid of the *itiriti* leaf box.

But every day, the light keeper opened the *itiriti* box, so that he and the young woman could enjoy themselves in the light. They laughed and played sweetly as honey wine.

But it happened that one day the young woman remembered she had to return to her father and bring to him what he had sent her to find. The light keeper held the woman close. Then, as a present, he gave her the *itir-iti* box filled with dreams and light. "I want you to take this with you," he said.

The young woman found her father asleep in his

hammock. "Father," she whispered, "the *hebus* have left me safe, and I have brought you light."

The chief woke fully and welcomed her. She showed him the light trapped in the leaf box. He hung the box from one of the stilts that held up his house. Its dreams drifted out, and rays of the light touched the crinkled water of the Orinoco, the fan-shaped leaves of the *ite* palm, and the yellow-red fruits of the *merey.*

Word spread to all the neighboring villages that a family down the river had light. People traveled to see it for themselves. They arrived in their long purpleheart bark canoes, down this channel and that, boats and more boats, filled with people and more people.

Everyone packed themselves inside the house of the chief. They marveled at the light and at the new pictures that came while they slept. The man and his daughters fried fish after shimmering fish for their guests. Even their porch filled with people, until the slim stilts of the house could no longer hold the weight of so many. But since the light's clarity was so much more agreeable than the firelit darkness, no one left.

Finally, the chief could not stand so many people. "I am going to end this," he said. "We all want the light, so here it goes."

With a wonderfully strong toss, he hurled the *itiriti* box and its light into the sky. The body of the light flew to the East and the box rolled to the West. The body of the light became the sun. And the box, tightly woven of leaves as it was, turned into the moon.

On one side was the sun, and on the other, the moon.

But because the chief's throw had been so powerful, the sun and the moon moved very rapidly. The day and the night were very short, with sunrise and sunset following quick upon each other.

The chief had an idea. "Bring me," he said to his younger daughter, "a little turtle."

The young woman brought a small gray turtle cupped in her hands. The father blew on the turtle and then waited until the sun was just overhead. "Sun! I'm giving you a present!" he called out. "Take this turtle to be your friend. She is yours. I give her to you. Wait for her!" Then he took up his flute.

The little turtle journeyed up to the sun, the sweet notes of the flute warbling beneath her. And because turtles do not hurry, Sun had to wait a long time for his gift. When Turtle finally reached him, Sun walked very slowly across the sky so that he might keep step with his new companion. Moon ambled across the sky so as not to interrupt the beginning of this new friendship.

And to this day, when Sun gets up in the morning, almost always he travels at Turtle's pace, so that the day lasts just long enough until the night comes to the world by the Orinoco River.

La Befana and the
Royal Child of Light

Italy is the cradle of the vastly successful syncretism of peasant customs, imperial Roman holidays, and the Catholic Church's Christianity. Buon Natale *in today's Italy honors both the birth of Bambino Gesu and the "Unconquered Sun." In the early part of the common era's first millenium, an age of fascination with the idea of one god rather than many, the followers of Mithra, the Rising One, and Gesu, the Light of the World, vied for political and religious ascendancy.*

The Church borrowed Mithra's December 25th birthday, folded much of his imagery into the Gesu story, and studded the new Christ's Mass with symbols and celebratory elements from the old peasant revels and the midwinter feasts of Saturnalia and Opalia. The yule log, for example, lit ablaze to clean out the old year and to vitalize the new, was the most ancient of countryside customs and central to the Imperial Roman feasts. And now at each hearth's fire, it is said, Gesu's mother Mary enters and warms there her newborn child.

By the twelfth and thirteenth centuries, when litera-

ture began for the first time to be written not just in Latin but in the languages of ordinary people, Italy was a treasure box of tale and legend. The best known legend of today's Italy, the story of La Befana, marries religion and food, the flour and butter of this rich culture. La Befana, the witch-fairy, whose name means "epiphany," was once reviled with rude songs, thudding earthern-ware bells, and shrill trumpets. But the people had their own epiphany, and today children eagerly await this old woman as she flies each year, on January 6, the Feast of the Three Kings, from the Alps to Sicily, looking for the Royal Child of Light. She carries with her cakes with candied fruits and gingerbread made with hazelnuts, almonds, and honey. The nuts honor earth's fertility, and the honey teaches the baby new year to be sweet.

La Befana and the Royal
Child of Light

LA BEFANA IS a tall old woman
with a red shawl and a bent branch
broom that goes sweep-swep-
sweep. She lives in a thin wooden
house with a round-topped door in
the shadows of the dark purple mulberry trees. La
Befana sweeps the mulberry leaves, sweep-swep-sweep,
into piles. Crunch-crackle-crunch.

La Befana has a long nose and a hump on her back.
Her hands are speckled with pale chocolate. She pins
the white billow of her hair with bone combs. Befana's

kitchen shelves are libraries of jars and tins. Honey, almonds, hazelnuts, and the skins of lemons and tangerines. Cloves, vanilla beans, and cinnamon. Hills of sugar and silky flours, with chipped china teacups for scoops.

Up until the winter of our story, La Befana had swept and baked for no one but herself. Sweep-swep-sweep went her broom, year after day, day after year. Spicy, doughy smells curled out of her windows as she baked: beat-bet-beat, knead-knod-knead went her hands. Clack-drack-clack went the sticks for her stove.

La Befana never spoke. People heard her noises, but they never heard her voice. At least, people could not remember the last time they had.

But one year in wintertime, when the leaves dried in yellow-brown piles, Befana had a conversation. Everyone heard her. And then, La Befana's story changed forever.

One fine morning, a strange parade marched down the mulberry street. Everyone watched, shouting and crowding at the edges of the procession. La Befana stayed inside, but she parted her curtains and stared.

She saw enormous, clopping brown beasts with knobbed knees and bumps on their backs. Cases carved with suns and crescents thumped the sides of the brown giants with each huge mincing step they took. Jewel-colored flags. Old man in red turban at the front; a younger, head in a pillow of purple, at the middle; and a third, robes green as orange tree leaves, at the rear. A boy jigging to the song of a stringed box, another shaking a belled stick with red ribbons.

Befana's breath frosted her window. She rubbed it clear with her fingers. At that moment—everyone saw it—a child sprinted out of the throng straight to Befana's door. He hopped from foot to foot there, knocking—knock-kneck-knock—at her door.

La Befana cracked the door, then opened it wide enough to show herself, her hand clutched around her bent branch broom. The music stopped. The parade paused. It was as if even the strangers knew that La Befana needed silence to try out her words.

Everyone saw the little boy reach for the hand that held the broom. People saw La Befana's hand tighten on the old bent branch. But she gave him her other hand, closing his little one in her own.

People puffed with breath they did not let out.

The child spoke first.

"We're looking for the Child of Light, Nona. We're looking for the Royal Child who will light up the world."

People's breaths went out and in.

"Eh?" said La Befana.

"We're looking for the Child of Light, Nona. Come with us. We're bringing the Royal Child our gifts."

La Befana was silent.

"Come, Nona," said the boy.

And then La Befana spoke, voice husky with years of no use.

"I have my sweeping," she said.

"Come," said the boy.

"I have my baking, child," said La Befana. "I have to gather the wood."

And then the boy wrapped his arms round her gray skirts and clung. Everyone watched La Befana set away her broom. La Befana rested both old hands on the child's small back.

Then somewhere in the clear air the music started again. Like dancers, the people and the animals in the parade pivoted, began to jostle, to call out to one another.

The boy unstuck himself and plunged away. La Befana stood for moments before she clenched her broom and shut her door hard.

If you had been listening at her door, you would have heard the sounds again of that bent branch broom. Sweep-swep-sweep, sweep-swep-sweep. But the sound would have smudged a little: Sweep, swep, swep. Swep. Swep—as if La Befana were leaning and thinking.

If you had peeked in the window, you could have seen her dreaming there, leaning on the broom. Her eyes like chocolate melting; tiny images of La Befana mirrored again and again in the library of kitchen jars, now very still. Then, suddenly, La Befana and all the mirrored La Befanas began to move. And all around, the kitchen moved, too.

Lids clattering from tins. The rolling pin dancing. Eggs bursting themselves in red and green bowls. Beat-bet-beat, knead-knod-knead. Cloves and cinnamon swirling through the air. Rinds of lemons and oranges scattering like commas and parentheses onto pages of rolled out flour. Vanilla beans shivering in snowy sugar. Almonds and hazelnuts cavorting in honey. Cream frothing. Chocolate slivers spinning from the backs of La Befana's hands. Drifting onto balls, twists, and mezzaluna rolls of cookies and cakes. The hot oven mouth closing on them all.

Then, in a careen of perfume, La Befana packed a basket. Layer after layer, lie-lo-lee, of cookies, cakes, and candies.

Then—are you watching?—La Befana smoothing her hair and pinching her combs tight. Pinning her red shawl at her throat. Resting her fingers on her eyes. And finally, taking up the basket and opening her door.

La Befana has her gifts for the Royal Child. But it is twilight now, and a red ribbon on the street is all that is left of the parade. Can La Befana catch up? A mulberry leaf settles like a crown at her feet.

La Befana disappears and returns with her broom. She begins to run. The basket bounces at her side. She wheezes. She runs and runs, and then, suddenly, a gust catches her. The broom tilts and lifts. La Befana flies away up high into the stars.

La Befana is a tall old woman with a bent branch broom that goes sweep-swep-sweep. She lives in the shadows of the mulberry trees, and she bakes and gathers wood and talks not much at all. But ever since that winter, La Befana packs every year a basket of gifts—cookies, cakes, and candies—for the Royal Child of Light.

La Befana never catches up to the parade. But she

flies each year across the sky, stopping at every house below. She is looking for the Child who will light up the world. La Befana is never sure what the Child may look like. So she leaves her gifts at every home, in case the girl or the boy within is the Royal Child of Light.

Rites and Games for Winter Solstice Nights

Shut off the electricity. Read, sing, and play by candlelight.

Tree Offering

Sprinkle seeds, glitter, or cornmeal at the foot of a tree outside.

Leaf to leaf, root to root, seed to seed:
may all that we have be all that we need.

Cutting the Deadwood

Prune the dead branches from a tree outside.

Deadwood, deadwood cut away—
Strength and blossom come to stay!

DECK THE HALLS

Decorate the house with cuttings of rosemary, bay, holly, ivy, fir. Everyone names a blessing for the year. Sing *Deck the Halls* (see songs).

BAKE AND EAT A TREAT

Into the oven we slide this treat
May all hold close and life be sweet!

PILE ON THE LIGHT!

Remove one chair each round of music as in the old game of Musical Chairs. But, instead of players dropping out, as in the old game, the task is to fit more and more players onto fewer and fewer seats!

GIVE AWAY

Each person chooses an object in the room to which they assign the meaning of what they are letting go this new year.

(I *"give away"* *this clock because I give up wasting time.*)

Now each person "receives" someone else's object, to which they assign the meaning of what they want to have more of this new year.

(I'll take your clock because I want more time to relax!)

I Am

Each person plays another life form and speaks a wish for all.

(I am Squirrel—I wish you planning ahead!
I am Dog—I wish you patience and happy walking!)

Topsy-Turvy

I'll be you and you be me! Grownups and children change places. Older children change places with younger; partners with partners.

Make a Play

Turn one of the solstice stories into a play. Use simple props and costumes—scarves, paper bags, signs taped to characters. A grownup or older child narrates. Children play parts.

DARK VS. LIGHT

Stage a fight between Night and Day with pillows or foam boppers.

Dark and Light
Dark and Light
Let strong young Day kill off old Night!

HOUSE LUCK

Hang the mistletoe. Shout three times:

Hug and kiss, hug and kiss
May this whole house be full of bliss!

SOLSTICE SONGS

Sung to the tunes of Christmas carols by the same names

DECK THE HALLS

(A traditional carol which predates Christian references. The yule is the time of year, but also a large log set afire to "teach" the light to return.)

Deck the halls with boughs of holly
Fa la la la la la la la la
'Tis the season to be jolly
Fa la la la la la la la la
Don we now our gay apparel
Fa la la la la la la la la
Troll the ancient Yuletide carol!
Fa la la la la la la la la

See the blazing Yule before us
Fa la la la la la la la la
Strike the harp and join the chorus
Fa la la la la la la la la
Follow me in merry measure
Fa la la la la la la la la
While I tell of Yuletide treasure!
Fa la la la la la la la la
Fast away the old year passes
Fa la la la la la la la la
Hail the new, ye lads and lasses
Fa la la la la la la la la
Sing we joyous all together
Fa la la la la la la la la
Heedless of the wind and weather
Fa la la la la la la la la

SILENT NIGHT

Silent night, holy night
All is calm, all is bright
Radiance streams from sun's infant face
Birthing again, you flood us with grace!
Bright star, light up the world!
Bright star, light up the world!

JOY TO THE WORLD

Joy to the world
The light returns!
Let folk their songs employ
While fields and floods,
rocks, hills, and plains
Repeat the sounding joy
Repeat the sounding joy
Repeat, repeat the sounding joy!

OH COME ALL YE PEOPLE

Oh come, all ye people,
joyful and triumphant
Oh come ye, oh come ye,
to the edge of the sea.
Come and behold it
Light this day returns to us.
Oh come let us rekindle
Oh come let us rekindle
Oh come let us rekindle:
Light returns.

O HOLY NIGHT

Oh holy night!
The stars are brightly shining!
It is the night of the Sun Child's birth.
Long we have lain in cold
and fear of hunger
But Sun returns
And the Earth wakes again!
A ray of hope:
The weary world rejoices
For yonder breaks
A new and glorious morn!
Sing and give thanks
Oh lift your voices high now
The Sun returns
Sun returns
to light the world.
Rejoice! Rejoice!
Oh Sun returns!

BIBLIOGRAPHY

Abraham, Ralph, Terence McKenna, and Rupert Sheldrake. *Trialogues at the Edge of the West: Chaos, Creativity, and the Resacralization of the World.* Santa Fe: Bear & Co., 1992.

Belting, Natalia. *The Long-Tailed Bear and Other Indian Legends.* New York: Bobbs-Merrill Co., 1961.

Bernstein, Margery, and Janet Kobrin. *The First Morning: An African Myth.* New York: Charles Scribner's Sons, 1972.

Bessire, Mark H. C. *Sukuma Culture and Tanzania.* photo.net/sukuma/intro.html

Carpenter, Frances. *The Elephant's Bathtub: Wonder Tales from the Far East.* New York: Doubleday & Co., 1962.

Cathon, Laura, and Thusnelda Schmidt. *Perhaps and Perchance: Tales of Nature.* New York: Abingdon Press, 1962.

China: Minority Nationalities. http://lcweb2.loc.gov/cgi-bin/query/D?cstdy:3:./temp/~frd_ZK9O::

Cosner, Sharon. *The Light Bulb.* New York: Walker, 1984.

Courlander, Harold. *The Tiger's Whisker and Other Tales and Legends from Asia and the Pacific.* New York: Harcourt, Brace & Co., 1959.

Craig, Robert D. *Dictionary of Polynesian Mythology.* Westport, Conn.: Greenwood Press, 1989.

Cunningham, Caroline. *The Talking Stone: Being Early American Stories Told Before the White Man's Day on this Continent by the Indians and Eskimos.* New York: Alfred A. Knopf, 1939.

D'Aulaire, Ingri and Edgar. *D'Aulaire's Norse Gods and Giants.* New York: Doubleday, 1967.

De Paola, Tomie. *The Legend of Old Befana: an Italian Christmas Story.* New York: Harcourt, Brace, & Jovanich, 1980.

Edgerton, Robert B. *Mau Mau: An African Crucible.* New York: Free Press, 1989.

Elwin, Verrier. *Tribal Myths of the Orissa.* New York: Oxford Univ. Press, 1954.

Fitzgerald, C. P. *China: A Short Cultural History.* New York: Praeger Publishers, 1972.

Gleik, James. *Chaos: Making a New Science.* New York: Penguin, 1987.

Grimal, Pierre, ed. *Laurousse World Mythology.* New York: G. P. Putnam's Sons, 1963.

Grousset, René. *The Rise and Splendor of the Chinese Empire.* Berkeley: University of California Press, 1953.

Haviland, Virginia, ed. *North American Legends.* New York: Collins, 1979.

Helfman, Elizabeth. *The Bushmen and Their Stories.* New York: Seabury Press, 1971.

Hood, Peter. *How Time is Measured.* Oxford: Oxford University Press, 1969.

Hull, Robert. *Norse Stories.* New York: Thomson Learning, 1993.

Hume, Lotta Carswell. *Favorite Children's Stories from China and Tibet.* Rutland, Vt.: Charles E. Tuttle Co., 1962.

Hyde, Lewis. *The Gift: Imagination and the Erotic Life of Property.* New York: Vintage Books, 1979.

Jenkins, Orville Boyd. *The Luhya of Kenya.*
http://www.grmi.org/jhanna/obj27.htm

Johnsgard, Paul A. *The Hummingbirds of North America.* Washington, D.C.: Smithsonian Institution Press, 1983.

Kaplan, Irving. *Tanzania: A Country Study.* Washington, D.C.: American University Press, 1978.

Langlois, John D., ed. *China Under Mongol Rule.* Princeton: Princeton University Press, 1981.

McDowell, Robert E., and Edwards Lavitt. *Third World Voices for Children.* New York: Odakai Books, 1971.

Manning Sander, Ruth. *A Book of Charms and Changelings.* New York: E.P. Dutton & Co., 1971.

Melzack, Ronald. *The Day Tuk Became a Hunter and Other Eskimo Stories.* New York: Dodd, Mead, & Co., 1967.

———. *Raven: Creator of the World.* Boston: Little, Brown & Co., 1970.

Miles, Clement A. *Christmas Customs and Traditions, Their History and Significance.* New York: Dover Publications, 1976.

Nilsson, Christopher. *Edgar Allan Poe's "The Raven".* www.poedecoder. com/essays/rav

Osborne, Mary Pope. *Favorite Norse Myths.* New
 York: Scholastic, Inc. 1996.
Philip, Neil. *Odin's Family.* New York: Orchard Books,
 1996.
Ponting, Clive. *A Green History of the World: The
 Environment and the Collapse of Great Civilizations.*
 New York: St. Martin's Press, 1991.
Radin, Paul. *The Trickster: A Study in American Indian
 Mythology.* New York: Schocken Books, 1972.
Rasmussen, Knud. *Eskimo Songs and Stories.* New
 York: Delacorte Press, 1973.
Seed, Jenny. *The Bushman's Dream: African Tales of the
 Creation.* Scarsdale, N.Y.: Bradbury Press, 1974.
Shostak, M. *Nisa: The Life and Words of a !Kung
 Woman.* New York: Random House, 1981.
Skutch, Alexander. *The Life of the Hummingbird.* New
 York: Crown Publishers, 1973.
Thompson, Vivian L. *Maui-Full-of-Tricks.* San Carlos,
 Calif.: Golden Gate Junior Books, 1970.
Tribals of Orissa. www.orissa-tourism.com/tribals.htm
Vittorini, Domenico. *Old Italian Tales.* New York:
 David McKay Co., 1958.
Wilcock, John. *Traveling in Venezuela.* New York:
 Hippocrene Books, 1979.

Wright, Lawrence. *Clockwork Men: The Story of Time, Its Origins, Its Uses, Its Tyranny.* New York: Horizon Press, 1968.

ABOUT THE AUTHOR

CAROLYN McVICKAR EDWARDS, author of *The Storyteller's Goddess*, is haunted by an old Gaelic-speaking storyteller's tears as he told of television's grip on the families of his town. Joel Chandler Harris, the collector of Uncle Remus tales, was one of her childhood heroes. Her own work seeds folk ways—in which ordinary people make their own entertainments for each other—in written and oral literacies: in books, face-to-face conversations, storytelling, and folk songs.